KICK THE BUMS OUT!

KICK THE BUMS OUT!

THE CASE FOR TERM LIMITATIONS

Americans to Limit Congressional Terms

National
Press
Books

Washington, D.C.

Library of Congress Cataloging-in-Publication Data

Coyne, James K., 1946-
Kick the bums Out!:
The Case for Term Limitations
160 p. 15 x 23 cm
ISBN 0-915765-85-3: $9.95
1. United States. Congress--Term of office
I. Title. JK1140.C693 1992
328.73'073--dc20   92-19085
                          CIP

Dedication

Someday, a newly-elected member of Congress will raise his or her hand to take the oath of office and not be thinking about getting re-elected.

Someday, a member of Congress will cast a vote with the next generation in mind, not tomorrow's headline.

Someday, a member of Congress will decide that it is better to worry about raising our nation's ethical standards than raising funds for television ads.

Someday, a member of Congress will worry as much about protecting the taxpayers' checkbooks as protecting his own.

Someday, members of Congress will be ordinary citizens, not professional politicians.

Someday, Americans won't be screaming: Kick the Bums Out!

This book is dedicated to that day.

Acknowledgments

Americans to Limit Congressional Terms acknowledges the Founding Fathers of this nation, especially Thomas Jefferson, for their belief in limited terms for members of Congress.

Credit must also go to the modern-day patriots who have helped lead the fight to limit congressional tenure. In particular we want to acknowledge the contributions of Jim Coyne, Ed Crane and Cleta Mitchell, who not only have served on the board of ALCT, but also contributed to this book.

We also want to thank Kristine Kirby, communications director for ALCT, for her help in assembling much of the information in this book. Her enthusiasm, and commitment to this project were critical to its success.

Finally, we want to acknowledge the assistance of all those who participated in our Congressional Forum on Term Limits in May, 1992, and especially the leaders of the state term limits organizations who are working so diligently to put term limits referenda on the ballots of their states. Without the support of hundreds of thousands of individual members and supporters ALCT would not have been able to publish this book. To all of them we say "Thank you."

Contents

Foreword

by Jack Anderson

Mr. Anderson's syndicated column "Washington Merry-Go Round," is published in 1,000 newspapers. He is author of a dozen books including The Cambodia File, The Confessions of a Muckraker and Fiasco.

Americans everywhere are fed up—sick of a government that doesn't work. Washington has become a synonym for waste, corruption and deceit. None of our elected officials ever accepts responsibility for the state of our nation, the economy, the infrastructure, the schools, or the efficiency and cost of government itself. It's always someone else's fault. Some brazen politicians pass the ultimate buck—they blame the voters. Now the voters are angry!

This book is about those voters, the American electorate, and what they are doing to take control of government again. It explains the who, what, why, how and when of the most important campaign for political reform in over a century: the campaign for term limits. It is a story of the second American Revolution.

For more than four decades I have watched Washington. Throughout it all, one theme has been constant: Power corrupts.

Human nature is no different today than it was during the McCarthy hearings in the '50s, the "trial" of Adam Clayton Powell in the '60s, the Abscam cases of the '70s or the Keating Five scandal of recent years. Powerful politicians always try to put themselves above the law and will do almost anything to get more power, fame and fortune. It comes, it seems, with the territory.

The Founding Fathers understood human nature and our need to protect ourselves from the ambition of politicians. To shield us from the inevitable tyranny of entrenched officeholders, they placed their faith in a unique new political institution—a citizen legislature called Congress, where regular elections would ensure that ordinary citizens would hold office only for a short period of time.

We were to be the first country whose leaders would not be rulers. Citizens, that is—the ruled, would be elected to Congress, and a widely acknowledged principle of rotation in office would guarantee that members of Congress would not become lifelong legislators. The tyrant was not welcome.

Regular elections, together with the principle of rotation, worked well for more than a century. But the communications revolution of the 20th century changed the reality of popular politics and gave incumbent politicians new powers to exploit. Slowly, over the past 50 years, I have watched the impact of this new technology on politics. The result is a new breed of congressman: the professional.

Technology changed politics in two ways. First, the power of electronic media, beginning with radio in the '20s and '30s, brought Americans much closer to their President.

Sitting around the family's Atwater-Kent or RCA radio console, they heard, most for the first time, the voice of their president. A few years later in weekly movie newsreels, they would see their nation's chief executive standing on the White House steps. After the Second World War, television brought the Oval Office into their living rooms. Thus, they became personally connected with the president—and started to ignore Congress.

But Congress also learned to use new technology for its own benefit. By the mid-'70s, television and computerized word processors had become the incumbent congressman's most important political allies.

Elections are won today by 30-second negative television ads and blizzards of computerized political junk mail. The voter is manipulated with "scientifically tested" messages produced by an army of media specialists and PR consultants. No wonder he feels alienated by the whole political process. No wonder a revolution is at hand.

The fight to limit congressional terms is a struggle to put the voter back in control again. For decades he has pleaded with Congress to make elections fair, eliminate the abuses of incumbency and punish those who cheat and corrupt the system. But matters have only gotten worse.

The current scandals in Congress, from the House Bank overdrafts to the post office stamps-for-cash scam, reveal how arrogant and dishonest the members have become. The public knows they can't be trusted to clean up their own house—the only solution is to "Kick the Bums Out."

Americans to Limit Congressional Terms (ALCT) is the national grass-roots organization leading the term limits movement. Launched in 1989 when James Coyne and 32 other former Congressmen declared that Congress was becoming another House of Lords, it now has over 200,000 members across the country.

It is their idea to produce this book and help citizens everywhere understand the term limits issue. They asked leaders of the term limits movement—James Coyne, Ed Crane and Cleta Mitchell—to present the arguments and logic of term limits. *Kick the Bums Out* is the result. To me, it's a very convincing case.

This book presents the whole story of term limits—where the idea came from, where it's going and a rebuttal of the arguments used against it. It also offers the committed reader a guide for his own involvement in the term limits campaign.

And if ever there was a political campaign worthy of individual involvement, this is it. Term limits will revitalize Congress and our whole government.

For decades, frustrated Americans have been trying to change Congress one member at a time. These days, new blood comes into Congress only when death, retirement or scandal provides an opening. Term limits will insure that new faces, new minds, new ideas, new programs and new energy come into Congress every two years.

But even more importantly, term limits will bring a new kind of person to Congress— citizens who have other careers and don't want to be congressmen-for-life. They'll be people who understand what the real world is like: where checkbooks must be balanced, where postage isn't free, where laws must be obeyed, and where there isn't a bottomless pit of money at their disposal.

The last chapter of *Kick the Bums Out!* gives you a list of ten things you can do to help limit congressional terms. I hope that you will decide to join this crusade. It doesn't matter if you're a Democrat, Republican or independent—it only matters that you want a better Congress. If you do, the term limits movement needs your help.

Read this book carefully. Consider all that needs to be done. Look at the mess in Washington and at the entrenched politicians who sit in Congress today. Look at their power, their perks and their privileges.

Then, look at your own family and friends. Consider what kind of future America is facing. What will the 21st century mean to the next generation of Americans? More deficits? More decline? More confusion and unaccountability in Congress?

We can't wait for someone else to rebuild our government and restore the principles that once made it great. No single person can be America's political savior—no single congressman, senator or president. The answer lies with the whole institution of government and with ourselves. We've got to take control again. We've got one thing to do first: **Kick the Bums Out!**

Chapter One

The Second Declaration of Independence

If Thomas Jefferson were to return to America today, his heart would sink. The citizens don't vote, the government is unaccountable and the Congress is corrupt.

Surely he would lead the fight to reform, arguing, as he did 200 years before, that we need to restore our Citizen Legislature. If so, he would probably begin with an eloquent plea for revolutionary change—something like this:

When in the course of events, it becomes necessary for one people to dissolve the political bonds which have connected them with another, they should declare the causes which impel them to separation.

We hold these truths to be self-evident, that all men and women are created equal, that they are endowed with certain inalienable rights, that among these are life, liberty and the pursuit of elective office.

To secure these rights, governments are instituted among men and women deriving their just powers from the consent of the governed. The governed are withdrawing their consent from Congress because Congress no longer represents the governed; Congress only represents *itself*, evidenced by the decline of the United States, the never-ending increases in the federal deficit, coupled with huge pay raises for members of Congress.

Whenever any form of government becomes destructive of these ends, it is the right of the people to alter or abolish it, and to institute new government, laying its foundation on such principles and organizing its powers in such form, as to them seem most likely to effect their safety and happiness.

The Constitution has served the Nation well. After more than 200 years, there have been only 27 amendments. Based on this document, America grew to become the most powerful and influential nation in the world. Now, America is on the decline, like Great Britain before it. One of the reasons for the decline is the stagnation and collapse of our Congress.

Congress has become the great bastion of the special interests. Examine the organizations and politicians who oppose term limitations and you will learn who owns Congress. It is time to refound our Congress and give it back to the people.

The history of the present Congress is a history of repeated injuries and usurpations, all having in direct object the establishment of an absolute tyranny over the American people. To prove this, let the facts be submitted to a candid world. Congress has refused to address the most important issues of our times:

Congress has failed to present a balanced budget in 20 years.

Congress has represented one generation at the expense of another.

Congress has taken contributions from directors of savings and loans and has allowed these same scoundrels to steal from the people.

Congress has failed to represent the interests of our soldiers and sailors who have given brave and loyal service to the defense of our country.

Congress has become beholden to lobbyists, and has represented the interests of large corporations and foreign governments rather than the American people.

Congress has used the privilege of the frank and other privileges of incumbency to ensure re-election at the expense of the people of the United States.

Congress has allowed our educational system to deteriorate and refused to allow the citizens to choose better schools for their children.

Congress has allowed our cumulative trade deficit for the past ten years to exceed the entire trade surplus since the nation was founded.

Congress has allowed the greatest nation on earth to become the world's largest debtor.

In every stage of these oppressions we have petitioned for redress in the most humble terms; our repeated petitions have been answered only with repeated injury. Princes (and Congress is now home to many of this ilk) whose character is thus marked by every act which may define a tyrant are unfit to rule a free people. We have appealed to their native justice and magnanimity, and we have conjured them by ties of our common kindred to disavow these usurpations, which would inevitably interrupt our connections and correspondence. They, too, have been deaf to the voice of justice and consanguinity. We must therefore, acquiesce in the necessity to confront the entrenched tyrants of Congress and hold them, as we hold the rest of mankind, enemies in war, in peace, friends.

We, therefore, the People of the United States of America, appealing to the President of the United States and the Congress, for the rectitude of our intentions, do in the name, and by authority of the good people of the United States, solemnly publish and declare that all political connections between the people and Congress are and ought to be totally dissolved until a constitutional amendment is passed allowing for the orderly transfer of power from one generation to the next, and that until that is done, it is time once again to separate from our designated rulers and **KICK THE BUMS OUT!**

Chapter Two

Introduction:
The Problem

According to the Gallup Poll, over 70 percent of the American public favors congressional term limitations. The problem is clear: Incumbents, good and bad, are re-elected 97 percent of the time in the House of Representatives, 82 percent by landslides. *The Wall Street Journal* a few years ago said, "The turnover rate among members [of Congress] is now lower than that of the Soviet Communist Party's central committee." We all know what happened in Moscow: The Communist politicians were kicked out. It's time to *kick the bums out* of Congress, too.

In 1990 an astounding **97 percent** of the incumbents were re-elected. Only six members of Congress lost their bids for re-election, and five of the six had been accused of unethical conduct. During the decade of the 1960s, 142 incumbents were defeated; in the 1970s, 97 were turned out by the voters; and in the 1980s, only 88 lost their House seats out of 2,175 races, and most of those were only defeated because of gerrymandering in 1982 or scandals like Abscam.

These numbers are important not only because they reveal how uncompetitive and unfair our elections have become, but also because of how they influence and reflect the behavior of our elected officials.

Congressmen live in a world where they are constantly running for re-election. They win their elections by raising millions of dollars from special interests. Before long, they lose touch with their constituents and assume the arrogance of royalty.

This explains, in part, their declining ethical and moral standards. After a few years in office, they are all-powerful and nearly unbeatable. They write the laws, but refuse to obey them. And worst of all, they refuse to accept responsibility for government—no one can hold them accountable because no one can force them out of office.

But now the people have rediscovered the wisdom of the Founding Fathers. Over two hundred years ago at our Constitutional Convention, they told us what to do. There is a way to "kick the bums out," and keep them out, they said: Limit their terms.

Congressmen for Life

First elected in 1941, 33 days before the invasion of Pearl Harbor, Representative Jamie Whitten of Mississippi has had his seat for over a half century, longer than any Representative in history. His long career as a professional politician is what every new Member aspires to. In the current Congress, most Members have served more than a dozen years, and one in five has been there for more than two decades.

They are, in short, entrenched. They've mastered the system. They are proud to call themselves political pros. They are congressmen-for-life.

Rotation in Office

A hundred and fifty years ago, congressmen served only a term or two and then returned to private life. In 1842, fewer than a quarter of all members of the new Congress had served in the previous one. We had what was then referred to as "rotation in office"–a tradition of voluntary term limits.

Andrew Jackson, the most famous president of the era, understood why term limits were so important:

> Every man who has been in office a few years believes he has a life estate in it, a vested right. This is not the principle of our government. It is a rotation in office that will perpetuate our liberty.

Unfortunately, politicians had forgotten Jackson's words a century later. Once they did, public confidence in our Congress began to collapse. Today, Congress is corrupt.

Congressional Exemptions

One measure of that corruption is the way Congress exempts itself from the operation of many of the laws it passes. Members don't have to obey the Civil Rights Act, the Equal Employment Opportunity Act, the Equal Pay Act, the National Labor Relations Act, the Occupational Safety and Health Act, the Freedom of Information Act, the Privacy Act and the Ethics in Government Act. Just recently, we've learned that they don't obey the federal banking laws either.

James Madison warned against such congressional exemptions during the Constitutional Convention:

> Congress can make no law that will not have its full operation on themselves and their friends, as well as on the great mass of society. This has always been deemed one of the strongest bonds by which human policy can connect the rulers and the people together. It creates between them that communion of interests and sympathy of sentiments of which few governments have furnished examples; but without which every government degenerates into tyranny.

Privileges of Incumbency

Another sign of Congressional corruption is the way members abuse the privileges of incumbency. Just one example is enough to illustrate their power to pervert our elections: the frank, member's right to mail propaganda to their constituents at taxpayer expense.

The average member of Congress sends out 12,000 pieces of mail for every one he receives. They will spend nearly $200 million this year sending truckloads of free junk mail

Reprinted with permission of King Features Syndicate.

to their constituents. Even worse, they now are using the frank to send mail outside their districts to reach future voters. And, as we shall see, this is only one of dozens of incumbency advantages they have. The result, of course, is that elections have become almost meaningless.

Voter Turnoff Instead of Voter Turnout

The voters don't like to be cheated and they don't like to waste their time. It isn't surprising, therefore, that so many have decided to ignore congressional elections.

A study by the Kettering Foundation concluded that "many Americans don't believe they are living in a democracy. They describe the present political system as impervious to public direction." As a result, most of them don't bother to vote.

In 1986, adjusting for gubernatorial and senatorial elections, only 27.6 percent of those eligible cast their votes for candidates for Congress. Voter turnout in the United States is lower than that in France, Israel, El Salvador, Italy, Latvia, Germany—lower than that anywhere in the world! Why vote when the average incumbent is getting 73.5 percent of the vote, 85 percent of Congressional incumbents get over 60 percent and 63 House members got more than 94 percent?

People don't vote because they think their votes don't matter. With incumbents virtually assured re-election, the reason to vote is greatly diminished.

But this year the voters have another choice! They can vote for term limits and add an amendment to the Constitution restoring this fundamental principle of a Citizens' Legislature.

Term limits will mean open elections with no huge incumbent advantage in most circumstances. Each candidate will have the *same* advantages. Better candidates will be willing to run. Voters will want to be involved and participation will improve.

Around the world, new countries are being created from the ruins of the Communist Empire. They are tasting freedom and flocking to the polls. Former subjects are now voters.

Term limits will have the same effect in America by restoring the fundamental importance of our Congressional elections. After all, our voters are no different. All they want is a choice and the freedom to vote for change.

Term limits will give them that—and much more.

Chapter 3

The People vs. the Politicians

The History of Limitations on Political Power

Nothing was more obvious to our Founding Fathers than the evils of political power. The arrogance of the British political system was a primary cause of the American Revolution and every American was aware that he had little control over his own political destiny. The Revolution was supposed to change all that.

Only a few months before the first shots were fired at Lexington, Americans read a prophetic speech in the English House of Lords by William Pitt the Elder. "Unlimited power is apt to corrupt the minds of those who possess it," he declared, anticipating by nearly a century the more famous maxim of Lord Acton: "Power tends to corrupt; absolute power corrupts absolutely." Americans understood his warning and soon applied these fundamental truths to the fabric of their new democracy.

From 1776 to 1789, America was governed under the rules laid down in the Articles of Confederation. Each state was suspicious of the power of national politicians, and so the principle of rotation was established to guard against the corruption of absolute power. Most states established very frequent elections for state legislatures, some as short as every six months, to remind politicians that they wanted a citizens' legislature . They took special care to establish a tight and short leash for delegates to the Confederation Congress by limiting the term of office to one year and providing that no delegate could serve more than three years in any six-year period.

These mechanisms were designed to ensure against a perpetual ruling class of lawyers, politicians, and legislators who might thus become unresponsive to their constituents' needs and desires. The provision limiting tenure was proposed by John Dickinson of Delaware and adopted by Congress as part of the Articles of Confederation on October 14, 1777.

A few years later, the Congress was faced with the first violation of these term limits when Samuel Osgood of Massachusetts was investigated for "tarrying beyond (his) appointed terms." Showing a commitment to enforcing their rules that is hard to find these days, Congress quickly declared Mr. Osgood ineligible to serve and demanded his withdrawal from the House.

In 1787, delegates met in Philadelphia to draft a new Constitution. Most of them agreed with the principle of term limitation established under the Articles of Confederation and many expected that similar limits on the tenure of congressmen would be included in the new governing document.

A principle draft of the new Constitution known as the Virginia Plan provided that members of the House of Representatives would be "incapable of re-election" for a period of time "after the expiration of their terms of service." However, the language limiting tenure was characterized "as entering into too much detail for general proposition" and deleted from the final draft.

The idea of limiting congressional terms surfaced again during the First Congress when Thomas Tucker of South Carolina introduced a bill to limit service in the House to six years in succession, along with a companion bill limiting and shortening Senate terms. Unfortunately, Tucker was unable to get the House to vote on his proposal.

For the next 150 years, limiting congressional terms was not much of an issue because the tradition became established that congressional service was intended to be a brief period of civic duty. As described by scholars with the Library of Congress, "it became customary to serve no more than four years in the House nor six in the Senate," and service in Congress was viewed as a temporary duty undertaken on leave from some other occupation.

The same tradition of rotation became well established in the Executive branch from the very beginning. On September 19, 1796, George Washington delivered his famous Farewell Address, declaring his opposition to an imperial presidency and refusing to yield to pressure for a third term in office.

For nearly 150 years our presidents honored this precedent, until Franklin Roosevelt broke the two-term tradition in 1940. But the cry for reform was loud and swift. Less than two years after his death, Congress passed the 22nd Amendment to the Constitution, which was subsequently ratified by three-fourths of the states and certified as part of the Constitution on March 1, 1951.

The American people had declared again their opposition to unbridled power and unlimited tenure. A 1951 editorial in the *Washington Post* expressed the prevailing opinion:

> The only basic reason for writing this additional restriction into the Constitution is the fear that in these days of big government and perpetual emergency, some future president with dictatorial tendencies might perpetuate himself in office indefinitely. Perhaps that chance is remote, but power-grabbing officials are common enough in both history and current world experience to warrant this safeguard.

But Roosevelt wasn't the only politician seeking to turn elective office into a lifelong career. The trend was becoming increasingly evident in Congress, as well.

Not once in the nation's first 110 years was the average length of service in an incoming House of Representatives more than four years (two terms). In 1896, for example, the average length of prior service was only 30 months, but the 20th century brought increasing longevity to congressional political careers. By the 1920s the average member had spent five years in Congress, and since 1950 the average tenure has never fallen below seven years. The 102nd Congress, elected in 1990, has raised the seniority of its members to an all-time high: the average incoming member had been in Congress for more than a decade!

And yet, the careers of other political officeholders are increasingly becoming subject to limited terms. In addition to the President and Vice President, 28 Governors face term limits—many, such as Virginia, are limited to just one term in office. Hundreds of mayors and city councils, including those in Kansas City, San Jose, Jacksonville, San Antonio and Philadelphia (whose mayor has had limited tenure since the 1700s) benefit from term limits. And now, the term limit movement has begun its move into the legislative branch.

No political office is more suited to limited terms than that of our state and federal legislators. No one has more opportunity for abuse of power than those who control the purse strings of our government—and who determine the resources available for their own re-election campaigns.

At the same time, because of their size, legislative bodies are unlikely to suffer when term limits force a significant fraction to retire each session. Legislatures are designed to be our most representative branch of government, and frequent rotation of their membership increases the chance that the changing needs and makeup of society will be reflected in the legislative chamber.

But unfortunately, no one is better positioned to block reforms like limiting terms than incumbent legislators. The recent history of the term limitation movement at the state and national level demonstrates clearly that they'll do or say anything to stay in office: lie, cheat, threaten, steal, and even bribe us with our own tax dollars. They pledge that their most important job is to listen to us, the voters; but when we demand reforms in the system that lets them stay in office forever, somehow they can't hear us. But though they may be deaf, they're not immortal, as voters are proving from California to Maine, Florida to Alaska.

The Modern Term Limitation Movement

The story of the modern term limit movement begins with the Congressional elections of 1988. Some would call it an ordinary political year with an uninspiring presidential campaign that was more about symbols than substance. Democrats declared that the issue was "competence" and Republicans countered with appeals to patriotism and questions about prison furloughs. The media, as usual, defined the election in terms of Presidential personalities and promises, leaving the public to judge Congressional incumbents and candidates on the basis of their own propaganda.

The result was the lowest turnout for any presidential election in history as voters drowned their frustrations in apathy. President Bush was elected by promising a "kinder, gentler" version of Reaganism. Some called it a landslide (but with only 54 percent of the vote). The real landslide was by congressional incumbents. In the House, only six (plus one in a primary) were defeated—an all-time low—and most of those lost only because embarrassing scandals or peccadilloes slipped into public view. Never before had 99 percent of Congress been re-elected!

The public knew it had been hoodwinked, especially when only weeks after the election Congress moved to boost its pay by nearly 50 percent. Suddenly the secret was out. These guys didn't work for us—we worked for them!

By the spring of 1989, anger at Congress was turning into all-out revolt. The facts of the monstrous savings and loan debacle were coming to light, and slowly the public was beginning to understand the magnitude of this monument to congressional greed and mismanagement. The Speaker of the House, the majority whip and five incumbent Senators were all accused of doing secret favors for corrupt savings and loan fatcats in return for millions in campaign donations and special gifts. "Congressional ethics" had become the new oxymoron joke, replacing "military intelligence" and "political science."

But most citizens who looked in disgust at this congressional malfeasance were confounded by their inability to clean up the mess. For decades, incumbents in both parties had given lip service to campaign or procedural reforms, but little of substance ever became law and, if it did, the legislation was riddled with loopholes. Everyone had begun to conclude that career politicians had invented an unbeatable re-election machine which had turned them all into Congressmen-for-Life. Even the most sympathetic observers, former members of Congress, had reached the inevitable conclusion. "Absolute power" had won.

Thus, in late spring of 1989, 33 former members of Congress formed Americans to Limit Congressional Terms (ALCT) and the modern term limit movement was begun. Democrats and Republicans together, they decided to lead a national debate on how to clean up Congress.

Their solution: Restore our Citizens Legislature through enactment of a constitutional amendment limiting the tenure of members of Congress. The response: a national grassroots revolution that includes millions of ordinary Americans dedicated to taking control of their Congress again.

The day before ALCT's first national news conference, word about the campaign spread across Capitol Hill. A *Roll Call* article that morning predicted that the movement would quickly gain momentum, and the *Wall Street Journal* declared its support in its lead editorial, alongside a list of the 33 courageous former members who had begun the fight.

Within a few months, 25,000 voters had joined Americans to Limit Congressional Terms, and affiliated groups in dozens of states were quickly established. By April 1990, thousands of petitions were being circulated to get the question on the ballot in Oklahoma, Colorado and California. Thus began the modern American Revolution to overthrow a ruling aristocracy and reassert popular control of our government—of the people, for the people, and by the people.

Oklahoma

On September 18, 1990, Oklahoma voters sent a message to the nation. Sixty-seven percent of the electorate voted for a 12-year limit on terms in the state legislature, the first time limit put on state or federal legislators since the Articles of Confederation in 1776, which limited representatives to three years of service out of every six years. The Oklahoma law is not retroactive, so current legislators can be elected for twelve more years.

Jack Gargan

In the summer of 1990 Jack Gargan, a 60-year-old retired financial planner from Tampa, Florida, reached into his pocket and paid for a series of newspaper ads. The full-page newspaper ads read:

> I am outraged . . . incensed, livid [and] not going to give in to these clowns!

His ads drew 70,000 contributors who donated $1 million, enough to finance another 240 full-page ads. Gargan started a one-man organization called THRO, Throw the Hypocritical Rascals Out. His 132-day campaign was popular, but did it accomplish anything? Voters re-elected 97 percent of members of Congress seeking to retain their seats in 1990. Those reelected, however, found their margin of victory narrowed considerably, some by more than ten percent.

Colorado

On November 6, 1990, Coloradans passed a comprehensive ballot initiative limiting terms of state officeholders and federal representatives to Washington. The terms of the governor, lieutenant governor, secretary of state, attorney general and state treasurer were limited to two consecutive four-year terms. State senators were also limited to two consecutive four-year terms, while state representatives were limited to four consecutive two-year terms.

United States Senators from the Rocky Mountain state were limited to two consecutive six-year terms. Representatives were limited to six consecutive two-year terms. The key provision of the Colorado law was the "consecutive" provision. This requirement forces long-term legislators to sit out four years, either by entering the private sector or seeking a different office. Because the limits are not retroactive, the constitutionality of the Colorado limit on federal officeholders' terms will probably not be decided by the courts for many years to come (because no one's term will be limited for years).

California

In 1990 California voters overwhelmingly approved a referendum limiting state legislators to serving for eight years in their lifetime. The California Supreme Court upheld voter-approved limits on the terms of state legislators by a vote of six to one. The United States Supreme Court has decided not to review the appeal of that case. The law does not apply to congressmen and senators from California serving in Washington, D.C.

Washington State

In 1991 Washington voters turned down, by a vote of 54 percent to 46 percent, a term limitation initiative. Opponents poured millions of dollars into the campaign to defeat the initiative. Representative Tom Foley, the Speaker of the House, who claims to provide special clout for Washington State, worked hard to defeat the initiative.

Momentum

Each of those three initial states was critical to the early success of the congressional term limits movement: Oklahoma because it was first and gave the campaign a critical shot in the arm early in the fall; Colorado because it combined state legislative limits with a bold new proposal to unilaterally limit Colorado's congressmen and U.S. senators; and California, because once an idea catches on in the most populous of all states, you can be sure that the rest of the country is not far behind. And, in fact, the campaign for term limits exploded across the country throughout 1991 and into 1992.

Goaded by examples of congressional corruption, ineptitude and arrogance like the Keating Five whitewash, the Clarence Thomas hearings, the midnight pay raise, outrageous new redistricting maps and the House check-kiting debacle, the public concluded that term limits were a long-overdue reform that couldn't wait. By Christmas 1991, term limitation organizations were in place in 35 states, ALCT membership was approaching 200,000, and Election Day, 1992 was looming as the Waterloo of career politicians.

Even as public support for term limits was reaching record levels (receiving over 80% approval in one poll), career politicians in Congress were refusing even to debate the issue. House Speaker Thomas Foley at first dismissed the whole idea as unrealistic and unworkable, scoffing at the concept of a congress run by amateurs.

As revelations about the mismanagement of the House Bank, restaurant and post office exposed Congressional professionalism to be nothing more than old-fashioned political patronage and self-dealing, the concept of an amateur Congress began to look better and better. Now, the public has concluded that only with a constitutional amendment limiting Congressional terms can it restore the concept of a Citizens Legislature whose members seek neither personal rewards nor special privilege from public service. It's a simple concept to most Americans: give us a legislature of ordinary people who are willing to serve in Congress not to advance themselves, but because they love their country.

Night has fallen.

The country---troubled by a lingering recession, stubborn unemployment, a widening gap between rich and poor--- slips into a fitful sleep.

Lo! Lights burn in the Capitol, where our elected leaders wrestle late into the night with the challenges gripping the nation.

Chapter Four

Give Us Back Our Congress

On May 4, 1992, the Second American Revolution was launched. The political equivalent of war was declared against Congress and the battle lines were drawn. What some might call a ragtag army of hundreds of thousands of unarmed citizens sent their representatives into the fortress of the imperial Congress and proudly presented thousands of petitions from the people of every state, asking that members of Congress end their tyranny and peacefully end their domination of our government.

The occasion was the first Congressional Forum on Congressional Term Limits. Americans to Limit Congressional Terms (ALCT) had invaded Congress, sponsored the forum and declared in a nationally broadcast news conference that it was time for Congress to confront the reality of the term limit movement. Never before had ordinary citizens been permitted to enter the hallowed halls of Congress and demand that the politicians there give up what they cherish most: their power and their careers.

Senator Hank Brown, from Colorado, who supports term limits and whose constituents have declared their Congressmen and Senators will be limited to twelve years in office, was the official host of the daylong forum in the Senate Hart Office Building. He, along with Congressman Bill McCollum and Senators Dan Coats and Larry Craig, dared to support the heresy of term limits. [Aready they were being called turncoats, but, they knew history was on their side.]

Senator Brown wanted Congress to debate the most important issue of the day: term limits. For months, the media, the press and other so-called political experts had been cataloging the collapse of the country's confidence in Congress. Never before had so many Americans declared their distrust of our most cherished national institution.

Hundreds of congressmen had been caught abusing their privileges in the House Bank scandal. New reports were being disclosed about how congressional leaders were breaking the law and then, trying to cover it up. On the floor of the House and Senate, everyone was looking for some place to hide.

Leaders of ALCT asked members of Congress to look, instead, at themselves: Look at how out of touch they had become, how self-centered and how quick to always blame someone else for the nation's problems. It was time, they declared, to change Congress. It was time for a revolution.

But Congress wasn't listening. Its members just didn't get it.

They hoped that by ignoring the term limits movement they could make it go away. The leadership blocked all efforts to have the question of a constitutional amendment debated, even at the committee level. They even went to court to try to keep the issue off the ballot.

But here in the Capitol complex, on May 4, 1992, the revolution had arrived. James Coyne, President of Americans to Limit Congressional Terms and a former congressman himself, presented the challenge: Vote on a term limits amendment to the Constitution or get out of the way! It was time to discuss term limits in the Capitol, even if congressional leaders were afraid to. It was time to debate the question on C-SPAN, even if the cameras in the House and Senate chambers couldn't see such a confrontation. It was time for the career politicians in Congress to hear the voice of the American people.

Mr. Coyne then announced that every member of Congress had been given a pledge form to declare support for or opposition to term limits. Senator Brown was the first to sign his pledge and promised to urge his colleagues to commit themselves to the issue.

Senator Brown also issued a challenge to all the members of the House and Senate to debate him on the question of amending the Constitution and limiting congressional terms. But no one accepted his invitation. The leadership of Congress had told everyone to hide.

Throughout the day, ordinary citizens, as well as experts on Congress, presented the case for term limits. Men and women, black and white, from the East and the West, young and old—their message was the same: Give us back our Congress. "Term limits will bring competition," they said. "It will encourage ordinary citizens to get involved, and we'll have thousands of better candidates willing to run."

These new people, they knew, would be less worried about "doing what you have to do to win re-election" and ready to "do the right thing." It was the only way to restore confidence in Congress and hope in our future.

At the end of the day, only a dozen Congressmen had signed their pledge. Within a few weeks, a few dozen more had joined the fight, but more importantly, the public had become aroused.

ALCT announced that afternoon the battle plan of the term limits revolution and invited everyone to join in. A phone bank was established to enlist volunteers, and within days, tens of thousands had written or called the new 800 number (6IS-ENUF) to sign up.

The strategy was simple: Force Congress to vote for a constitutional amendment to limit terms. With the help of a little political judo, the people would twist every arm in Congress and then go to the mat for term limits.

First, ALCT announced a two-pronged political strategy. One prong was a series of term limits referenda, the other prong was a candidate pledge program in advance of the upcoming congressional elections. Together, ALCT hoped to force a majority in Congress to bring the question of a term limits constitutional amendment to a vote.

Fewer than half of all states permit public referenda on questions like term limits, and it isn't an easy process. In each case, a state committee must be organized, a formal petition drafted and approved, and then the petitions must be circulated and thousands of signatures must be collected.

It would be so much simpler if Congress agreed to debate and vote on the question, but the imperial Congress, like any tyrant, wasn't going to relinquish its power gracefully or easily.

In all likelihood, 13 states would have term limits referenda in 1992. It was almost as if the people of a new "13 original colonies" were leading the revolution, and, in fact, each state's term limits committee was filled with the spirit of the Founding Fathers. They saw themselves as "Refounding Fathers" who were leading our nation back to its most cherished original principle: the citizens legislature.

In these states, the plan was to collect thousands of signatures, get on the ballot and then, let the people be heard—and what a shout for democracy it would be.

Never before had so many petitions been circulated across the country on a single issue. By June 1992, more than two million signatures had been collected on term limits petitions. It was an historic campaign.

In the end, millions of citizens across the country, including those in some of our largest states like Florida, California, Ohio and Michigan, will be able to vote for term limits.

The outcome is not in doubt: Term limits will pass.

At the same time, in each of these states, every Congressional incumbent and candidate will be forced to answer the $64,000 Question:

When the term limits referendum passes in your state, will you support the decision of your constituents and vote for a Constitutional Amendment on Term Limitation when it comes before Congress?

More than 150 people will be elected to Congress from those 13 states. They will go to Washington with a commitment for term limits. The revolution will be on its way.

In the non-referendum states, candidates and challengers will face the Term Limits Pledge. It could be the toughest political questions of their lives:

★ *Do you support term limits?*

★ *Will you vote for a Term Limits Amendment?*

★ *Will you help force the issue to a vote in Congress?*

Anyone who does not answer "Yes" to all three will find thousands of voters saying "No" to him or her.

Incumbents, with all their political action committee (PAC) money, pork, propaganda and paid staff, may still get re-elected, but this year, because of redistricting, retirements and all the scandals, there are more open seats than in nearly 50 years. That's why the candidate pledge program is so crucial.

Ninety percent of all challengers are expected to sign the pledge. Eighty percent of the candidates for open seats should do likewise. The result will be 100 new Congressmen and Senators who have promised to fight for term limits.

Next year, the Congress will become an historic term limits battleground. Congressmen from the term limits referenda states will be honor-bound by the actions of their constituents to support a term limits amendment. New members from other states will have promised in their campaigns to fight for limits. Many of the others will see the term limits train coming down the tracks and, after decades of deceit and dishonor, finally decide to do the right thing.

Eventually, the vote for term limits can become a truly redeeming moment for Congress. Some old hacks will see the chance to end their careers with honor. Sinister and selfish solons will grasp at one last chance to be statesmen.

It will be the turning point of the Second American Revolution.

Congress will have moved from its cold political winter at Valley Forge and triumphed over its own careerism. It will be an instant that history will long remember.

Perhaps, scores of years from now as visitors enter the Capitol and look beneath the dome at the giant murals of the nation's most significant moments, schoolchildren will surround the painting that shows when our Citizens Legislature was founded—the day Term Limits in Congress became law.

You can join Americans to Limit Congressional Terms by calling—

800-6IS-ENUF (800-648-3683).

Chapter Five

How Our Rulers Rule Forever

In 1776, Thomas Jefferson proposed a resolution in the Continental Congress which said that "to prevent every danger which might arise to American freedom by continuing too long in office" the members should be limited to two years in office. Nearly 25 years later, in 1799, Jefferson was even more explicit:

Offices [i.e. political offices] are as acceptable [i.e. desirable] here as elsewhere, and whenever a man has cast a longing eye on them, a rottenness begins in this conduct.

Jefferson's premonitions have turned into prophecy. Today, Congress is rotten to the core.

Though the techniques and political devices that modern politicians use to reap personal rewards and advantage could never have been foreseen in Jefferson's day, his fundamental understanding of human nature is as applicable in the 1990s as in the 1790s. He knew that the self-interest of politicians would grow when long tenure inflated their egos. He knew that the pleasures and perquisites of office would seduce incumbents and weaken their sense of public responsibility. He knew that career congressmen would try to rig the system and hornswaggle the electorate. He just couldn't imagine how—and how thoroughly!

Incumbents, Jefferson knew, get corrupted. In turn, they corrupt Congress. In the end, the whole system collapses. If it is to be fixed, as Jefferson tried to warn us, the fundamental weakness of our legislature must be corrected: Long tenure in office must be prohibited.

The Best Job in the World

In a moment of candor as he was leaving office in 1989, House Speaker Jim Wright of Texas described his Congressional career in stark and simple terms: "It's the best job in the world." Many retiring members, especially those who feel the anger of the electorate this year, are more circumspect, declaring that they hate the job and are tired of the work, the ridicule and the lack of respect. Don't believe them. Wright was right.

Today, our congressmen are America's legislative lords. They are the rulers of all they survey. They consider themselves the country's best and brightest, and they live a lavish life, at taxpayers' expense, that must turn Jefferson over in his grave.

Each of them has a personal staff with at least 22 attendants toiling for his re-election and responding to his or her every whim. Their huge expense budgets would make Leona Helmsley green with envy. Chauffeured cars, a whole fleet of military jets and offices with every modern comfort give them a lifestyle no other career could possibly provide. Congress, in 1992, costs the taxpayer over $2 billion.

Best of all, doors are always opened for them wherever they go. Free passes to the Super Bowl, Disney World or the Kennedy Center. The best seat someone else's money can buy. Never a speeding or parking ticket. Free upgrades to first class on commercial flights. Reserved parking spaces, just for them, at

Washington's National airport. No one else ever gets this royal treatment.

And when they travel overseas, away from pesty constituents and nosy reporters, the treatment becomes truly regal. Over there, they are officially called a CODEL, the State Department's acronym for Congressional Delegation.

CODELs get the red carpet treatment—and then some. Each member is given a special red passport that lets him avoid customs, duties and long waits in line. Everywhere he goes he is chauffeured by eager State Department officers. Every meal is a state occasion, whether a guest of another government, a well-heeled lobbyist or our own ambassador. Special events like the Paris Air Show turn into hedonistic extravaganzas for a flotilla of Congressional frequent flyers: party after party followed by private visits to all the top spots, from Versailles to the Opera. In its spare time, a CODEL takes the limousines on a side trip to the finest shops and boutiques.

These junkets and international trips are only the most superficial joys of service in Congress. More psychologically significant, perhaps, are the power trips that members take every day—the ones in their minds where the ultimate destination is arrogance and tyranny.

Surrounded all day by sycophantic staff, obsequious lobbyists and a worshipful news media, it's not surprising that our humble public servants in Congress evolve into egos on top of egos. Everyone they meet tells them how wonderful they are—how eloquent, how thoughtful, how high-minded. An army of publicists cranks out propaganda extolling their virtues, their energy and their wisdom. Soon, they start believing their own flacks.

One California legislator admitted to a reporter that after his first election, he would enter a room full of people and think, "I am the most important person in this room." Decades later, after long tenure had transformed him, he would enter the same crowded room and ponder, "I am the most important person who has *ever* been in this room."

Such self-delusion is truly a disease—a disease that destroys a congressman's perspective, his conscience and ultimately Congress itself.

Congressman-for-Life

A Congressman is mortal. He wants to hold onto the best things in his life: his job, his power, his privileges, his self-delusion. These things define his existence—he must keep them at all costs. His conclusion: Do whatever it takes to get re-elected forever!

And so, he learns to cheat.

Cheating may seem too harsh a description, but that is the simple truth. Incumbent congressmen get re-elected over and over because they cheat.

They even admit it—but they call it "the advantages of incumbency," as though a baseball team that made the opposing pitcher throw from second base might call it a "home field advantage." Whatever it's called, it's cheating.

What are these incumbency advantages? They are, in short, almost everything that Congressmen do. They are the central purpose of life in Congress: Spending our money so they can keep getting re-elected.

The first advantage is the PR advantage. (That's public relations, though it might also stand for *perpetual re-election.*) At least half of all resources inside Congress are devoted to PR.

The Power of the Frank

First, meet Frank. Frank is what Congressmen call all the free mail they can send out (as in, "We will never give up the frank.") Franked mail is their own personal re-election direct mail program—and we, the taxpayers, pay every penny.

The idea, at first, was simple. Members of Congress could write to their constituents without buying stamps. They would just write their name out in longhand where the stamp would ordinarily go, and the Post Office would deliver it—no problem.

The problem came later when the Xerox machine, the computer and the Autopen were invented. That's when Frank turned into Philip, as Congress *fills up* our mailboxes with propaganda, promises and public relations.

The political equation is simple. People like to vote for someone they know. To get known, an anonymous incumbent writes them a letter. Sends them a newsletter. Sends an invitation to a town meeting. Get them to write back. Write them again, over and over. Before long, they know you. Then, they'll vote for you, even though they don't know who you really are or how you really vote.

In a world where most people get their news from television, where television rarely says anything about challengers in congressional races, and where challengers have to buy their own stamps and usually can't afford many, the frank can almost guarantee re-election.

Special-Interest Extortion

But just in case the frank isn't enough, incumbent congressmen have an even more powerful advantage: extortion. They call it "special-interest fund-raising," but extortion is the proper term—and they've turned it into a "legal," almost-mandatory element of modern politics.

Once again, the mathematics is simple. Incumbents create hundreds of committees and subcommittees in Congress to ensure that almost everyone has a position of power over some well-financed special interest.

Banking committee members, for example, get to extort banks, insurance companies, brokerage firms and developers. Energy Committee members can extort environmental groups, oil companies and automobile manufacturers. House Ways and Means Committee members (the tax creators) can extort almost anyone.

The incumbents then hold dozens of fund-raisers every year to solicit funds from the company, union and special-interest PACs that are subjected to their committee oversight. Usually it's a reception for $300 to $500, sometimes more, but the message is always the same: "I'm going to be re-elected next year whether you like it or not, so if you want to be able to get in my office, send a check."

These extortionists will solicit hundreds of thousands of dollars to finance their campaigns, but many of them won't even have opponents. For them, most of the loot ends up in their own pocket.

For the rest, the money goes to buy the wonder-drug of politics: The 30-second television commercial.

Campaign consultants, the parasites of modern politics, prey on incumbents by promising that miracles will flow from these wondrous TV commercials—and they do. Ordinary Congressmen can be transformed into political giants. Public impressions can be reversed almost overnight. Perceptions that a politician is ineffective or out of touch can be forgotten in a few weeks. Television ads for a worn-out incumbent are like liposuction or silicone injections for a fading movie star: Spend enough in the right places and you can fool almost anyone.

Today, most incumbents outspend their challengers on TV ads by more than ten to one. The lesson of politics in the television age is clear: The one with the most ads wins.

Although incumbents dominate the mailbox and the idiot box, challengers can at least fight back, but there's one receptacle of modern politics that belongs exclusively to incumbents—the pork barrel. This is the consummate symbol of incumbent power and the greatest fraud of all. This is why America is getting fat!

Some budget analysts estimate that over half of all the money spent by Congress is a brazen attempt to buy votes—and every member is working to increase his purchasing power. Today's cynical career politician knows that every voter has his price. Some are impressed with a new highway, a park or veterans' hospital. Others prefer funding for a local museum, day-care center or research lab. And everyone falls for the fallacy that because of *their* incumbent's clout, they are getting more out of government than the rest of the country.

As a group, we're a bunch of suckers. The truth is that we are all paying for pork that we don't need and can't afford. We waste billions on surplus military facilities, redundant regional offices and unnecessary demonstration projects that are funded for only one reason: To get an incumbent re-elected. It's like a trick card game where everyone loses but the dealer, and he's playing with our money.

Those are the major incumbency advantages—free mail and public relations, PAC money for TV commercials, and pork—but there are scores of others. For example, incumbents have an army of staff members who are really just free campaign workers writing and giving speeches, doing research, managing political volunteers, promising favors and schmoozing with the special interests. They also have access to millions of dollars worth of private congressional facilities, computer equipment and other resources that they use for their re-election. Most observers estimate that all together, an average Congressman's incumbency advantages would cost a challenger over $2 million to duplicate if he could.

Thus, it's not surprising that incumbents keep winning. If it wasn't for retirements, redistricting and resignations in the face of scandal or indictment, we'd almost have a permanent Congress. In many parts of the country, we already do.

Virginia's congressional elections in 1990 are a striking example of how little competition we really have. Just imagine if Thomas Jefferson could have voted and seen what his revered democracy had produced. Virginians that year had the following choice for U.S. Senator: The Republican incumbent—there was *no* Democratic opponent. At the same time, the five incumbent Democratic representatives from Virginia had *no* Republican opponents!

How could *both* political parties in the state fail to find candidates to run in these important congressional races? The answer is simple: Parties are irrelevant. The real structure of modern congressional politics is not Republican vs. Democrat; it's incumbents vs. challengers, and usually the challengers don't have a chance.

A recent study by the Kettering Foundation reveals that most voters have almost given up on congressional elections. Only a quarter of eligible voters participate, and most of them feel that the whole process is rigged.

This year, however, voters are angry and pushing for reform. Candidates across the country are being forced to address this fundamental question: Will you support a constitutional amendment limiting your tenure in office?

The public is asking every challenger: Will you be a citizen legislator, willing to return and live under the laws you pass, or are you hoping to be a congressman-for-life? Incumbents are running scared for the first time in decades. Some—perhaps as many as 30 or 40—might even lose, but the rest know that their days of unlimited privilege and automatic re-election are over. Term limits will soon be a reality.

Chapter Six

AreTerm
Limits
Constitutional?

During the course of the Constitutional Convention in Philadelphia, Abigail Adams wrote to her husband John urging him to "Remember the ladies . . . " and warned that the women of the country were determined to "foment a rebellion" against any government that tried to exclude them.

Abigail Adams was unsuccessful in her plea, but her predictions of a rebellion may well be fulfilled some 200 years later—and not just by "the ladies." Citizens of this country from all walks of life, ladies and gentlemen, old and young, black and white, Northerners and

Southerners are angry, upset and determined to "foment a rebellion"—and to take into their own hands the effort to place limits on a seemingly endless, unlimited political establishment that increasingly permeates every nook and cranny of their lives.

In 1990, as we have seen, three states passed term limitations on elected officials: Oklahoma, Colorado and California. Oklahoma's ballot question dealt exclusively with state legislators, while California's included only state legislators and executive branch employees. Colorado's initiative included both state officials and members of Congress elected from Colorado.

The ballots were barely counted in California before the state legislature filed a lawsuit in February 1991 challenging the constitutionality of the limitations. Fortunately the California Supreme Court in October 1991 rejected the challenge and found the term limit initiative to be constitutional. In March 1992 the United States Supreme Court refused to hear the appeal and the California term limits became cast in stone. The Oklahoma Supreme Court also has confirmed that the term limitation law in that state is constitutional.

Nevertheless, one of the common arguments of term limits opponents is what they believe is their ultimate trump card: Term limits are unconstitutional. Congressman Larry Smith and Speaker of the House Tom Foley have even used your tax dollars to pay staff lawyers for the House of Representatives to prepare legal briefs arguing that term limitations are unconstitutional.

Does the Constitution Have any Provision Concerning Term Limits?

In order for something to be unconstitutional there must be a provision in the Constitution that forbids it. There is nothing in the Constitution which forbids states or voters from enacting limits on the length of tenure in office—even for federal officeholders from that state.

The cases involving term limits for members of Congress will be a type of case never before presented to the courts. This is clearly uncharted territory. The California and Oklahoma court decisions approving term limitation initiatives are strong precedents for courts to uphold similar limits in other states.

What About State-passed Limits on Congressional Tenure?

No state other than Colorado has ever attempted to limit the terms of federal representatives. Article 1, Section 4, Clause 1 of the Constitution gives the states the authority to set the "times, places and manner of holding elections for Senators and Representatives." Stephen Glazier, a Washington attorney who specializes in constitutional law, cites a number of cases that support the constitutionality of term limitations. In one of those cases, *Clements v. Fashing*, the United States Supreme Court ruled in 1982 that a Texas law that prohibited state officeholders from running for other offices was constitutional. Glazier also looked at the history of the 17th Amendment to the Constitution which provides for the popular election of senators. Prior to its enactment in 1913, several states had individually changed the manner of electing *their* senators. If states could do *that*, then surely they can limit congressional terms. Glazier concluded that state limits on federal terms would be constitutional (*Wall Street Journal,* June 19, 1990).

Terry Considine, the leader of the Colorado movement to limit terms, carefully considered the constitutional question before launching the initiative drive. Considine, a Harvard-educated lawyer, believes that the Ninth and Tenth Amendments to the Constitution give citizens the right to limit the terms of federal officeholders. The Ninth Amendment provides: "The enumeration in the Constitution of certain rights shall not be construed to deny or disparage other rights retained by the people." The Tenth Amendment states: "The powers not delegated to the United States by the Constitution, nor prohibited by it to the states, are reserved to the states respectively, or to the people."

Without doubt, the Tenth Amendment presents the strongest argument in favor of term limitations, since the power to limit terms resides in the states or the people because this right was not delegated to Congress.

If we go back to the days of those who wrote the Constitution of the United States, there was a widely recognized principle of rotation in office: that legislators would be citizens and that legislators would not be career employees of the state.

That principle is as valid today as it was 200 years ago. Term limits is not some radical legal theory, but a well-documented pillar of good governance widely respected by our Founding Fathers.

The Clearest Path Is With a Constitutional Amendment

Even though many legal scholars believe state legislation and initiatives can constitutionally limit congressional terms, everyone admits that the best and clearest path is to push forward with a constitutional amendment. Those of the Founding Fathers, including Thomas Jefferson, who argued in favor of mandatory term limits, were correct in their predictions of what would transpire without term limitations. As the custom of voluntary rotation in Congress has fallen by the wayside, it becomes necessary to write into the Constitution mandatory rotation in office.

As states pass individual term limitation initiatives, it will only strengthen the case for term limits that apply in *all* fifty states. Eventually, Congress will lose the die-hard opponents to reform—and a term limits constitutional amendment will become law.

The 22nd Amendment to the Constitution is a clear precedent. It limits the president to two terms in office. Without doubt, Americans have every right to place the same limits on the careers of members of Congress.

Chapter Seven

There's No Accounting for Congress:

The Story of the House Bank

The American public uncovered Congress' fatal flaw in the fall of 1991. Lurking in a long-ignored safe in the House Bank was a symbol of decades of congressional arrogance, greed and corruption. There, investigators from the General Accounting Office discovered a bombshell: Congressmen couldn't even balance their own checkbooks.

In fact, it was worse than that. Hundreds of congressmen had consistently overdrawn their House checking accounts, some by hundreds of thousands of dollars, and no one had heeded warnings to correct the whole sloppy system.

What is now known as the House Bank scandal has already proved to be the most traumatic congressional scandal since the Credit Mobilier fiasco in 1873. Dozens of House members have been forced to resign, many have lost primaries that would have normally been uncontested and scores face the prospect of having to actually campaign this year after decades of getting automatically re-elected.

Greed and Arrogance

The story of the House Bank is a tale of two sins: Greed and arrogance. Thus, it is a sad reflection of our modern Congress and a fable of how even the most powerful tyrants can be caught in a web of their own design.

Over a century ago, the House of Representatives established a private bank to save its members the inconvenience of having to walk several blocks to cash their paychecks. Of course, over the years this original purpose was forgotten, and the House Bank evolved into one of the many lavish perquisites of congressional life.

For decades, the House has offered banking and check-cashing services for all its members and employees through the Congressional Credit Union, which operates three modern facilities, complete with tellers, car loans, certificates of deposit, interest-earning checking accounts and cash-dispensing machines. But modern-day congressmen have become accustomed to special privileges—and one of their most revered privileges was their own private Bank.

And What a Bank It Was

Ordinary citizens can only dream of having an account at such a bank. This bank treated every depositor like a King—even if he didn't have a cent in his account. On the wall, alongside the elegant brass and marble fixtures of this opulent institution, hung the pictures of the 435 members of House who were provided the special privileges of this exclusive bank.

It was like a bank with 435 bank presidents. None of them ever had to wait in line. Not one was ever asked to show identification or wait while a balance was verified. None was ever told that he couldn't cash an out-of-state check or that his funds would be "on hold" for a week or so.

Members liked the other special features of the bank, as well. They liked never having to pay any bank charges—for checks, overdrafts, returned checks or anything else. They also loved the special checks, artfully engraved with the imprimatur of the House sergeant-at-arms. Many members recalled stories of check recipients being so honored to get official Congressional checks that they refused to cash them. These were, in short, checks with clout!

Enter the Auditors

But the special feature of the House Bank that caught the eye of the General Accounting Office auditors was the endless overdrafts. Twice the GAO complained to the speaker and the sergeant-at-arms. Twice they were told that abuses would be corrected and twice they were deceived. Finally, the rubber checks hit the fan!

On September 18, 1991, a GAO audit reported that House members had cashed more than 8,000 rubber checks in the previous twelve months. Some members had constant *negative* bank balances. The next day, *Roll Call*, a small newspaper that covers the news of Capitol Hill, broke the story. The public reaction was outrage and disgust. Here, at last, was an example of congressional greed and arrogance that every American could understand. Here was the smoking gun of the imperial Congress.

In early October, Congress offered its customary response to allegations of corruption and dishonesty: stonewall and coverup. Six hand-picked members of the Ethics Committee would investigate on behalf of Congress, but no names of abusers would be released. The plan was to quickly sweep the whole affair under the rug.

The next day, the Chairman of the Ethics Committee excused himself from the probe, admitting that he had "cashed at least one bad check." (The actual number was 551!)

Within weeks, it was clear that this was a scandal that touched the majority of Congress. Even the speaker admitted that he had cashed "bad" checks.

Passing the Buck

But as might be expected, they said it wasn't their fault. It was the bank's fault. The bank kept sloppy records. The bank didn't credit all deposits on time. The bank didn't tell them that they were in arrears.

The public watched in disbelief. They could only imagine what would happen if they tried the same excuses at their bank. Millions of Americans who had paid penalties for over-drafting their accounts suddenly understood the privileges that congressmen took for granted.

Congress doesn't have to live by the same rules everyone else endures. Congress doesn't have to worry about balancing its checkbook—or anything else. After all, Congress writes the rules—and usually exempts itself from the ones it doesn't like. Congress is, in fact, exempt from the Ethics in Government Act. And so, when it was caught in a scandal like the House Bank debacle, it could write its own rules and determine its own punishment—or no punishment at all.

Finally, on March 5, 1992, the Ethics Committee released its recommendations: The full House should vote to identify the 24 worst abusers. (Five had already retired.) Everyone else should be shielded, even though one of them, a powerful committee chairman, had written 851 bad checks.

For weeks it seemed that Congress was living in an ethical bubble. Everyone outside of Washington watched in disbelief. How could they attempt such a brazen coverup?

Finally, on April 18, 1992, Congress was forced to release more information. The names of all 303 abusers and the number of bad checks were disclosed. The scandal had exploded.

The issue was never just a question of a little perk for a few members, but now it had become a dramatic symbol of the degree of congressional arrogance and corruption. Anyone might understand and forgive a Congressman with a few bounced checks—but here were scores of Congressmen, each with huge staffs to look after such details as balancing their checkbooks, who had systematically abused their overdraft privilege hundreds of times. (See Appendix Two for a complete listing of Congressional overdrafts.)

The public isn't stupid. The American public knew what was going on. Members were kiting checks to get interest-free loans that saved them thousands of dollars. In some cases, no doubt, the money would let them make last-minute donations to their own campaigns in clear violation of election laws. In other cases, it allowed them to play the stock or real estate markets with other people's money. In any case, it was an abuse of the public's trust.

Public Funds, Public Trust

Several members, the House Speaker for example, said it was an overblown issue. No public money was lost, they claimed.

The whole bank, in fact, was operated with public money. Every employee was paid with public money (The annual clerical payroll was

KICK THE BUMS OUT!

over $300,000.) and one poor $53,338-a-year cashier did nothing all day but call congressmen to inform them of overdrafts. Every piece of marble, every inch of brass railing, every computer, every elegant furnishing—everything was paid for with public money. The public, in short, provided 435 members of the imperial congress with the most lavish bank their selfish minds could imagine. And it was all totally unnecessary.

There was absolutely no excuse for it. Every legitimate banking service they might require was available in the offices of the Congressional Credit Union, conveniently located on the basement level of their office complex a few yards from the terminus of the private subway that shuttles them to the Capitol to vote. But so it is with Congress. Privileges need no logic. Perquisites need no justification. The rulers need ask no one for permission.

The Investigation Continues

The story of the House Bank is far from over. Voters have yet to pass their final judgment on the careers of the worst bank abusers. More significantly, perhaps, allegations of criminal behavior have not been disclosed, indictments have not been handed down and trials have not yet begun. All these are yet to come as the Justice Department pursues its investigation of the affair.

Malcolm R. Wilkey, a retired federal appeals court judge, has recently been appointed to lead the investigation. Congress waits in nervous anticipation for his report and the indictments that are sure to follow.

In the meantime, Congress continues to sweep the issue under the rug and to misunderstand the dimension of public anger.

The public isn't upset about a few (tens of thousands) of overdrafts. It isn't even the waste of public funds and the arrogance and imperiousness of incumbents. It is instead a question of priorities.

"Why is it," they ask, "that Congress always finds the time and money to look after their personal needs, but somehow can't find the time, the energy and the self-discipline to do the real job of Congress?"

Congress doesn't balance the nation's check book. In fact, it doesn't even try.

Congress writes billions of overdrafts at the U.S. Treasury every year and doesn't give a damn where the money will come from to pay those debts.

Congressmen always have time to ensure that their re-election campaigns are well-financed and carefully organized, but never seem concerned about the financing and organization of government.

Checks and Balances

The House Bank scandal is a metaphor for Congress' lavish attention to members' personal finances and benefits while they ignore the financial health of our country. It is symbolic of the castle of privilege they have built for themselves while mindlessly arguing for greater taxes and sacrifice from the electorate.

Most of all, it is an illustration of the motto of the modern congressman: "Don't you know who I am?"

"I don't have to bother with details like overdrafts," you can hear them say. "Don't you know who I am?"

"I don't have the time to worry about some trivial GAO report on the House Bank. Don't you know who I am?"

"I'm too busy with my campaign fundraisers, a television interview and meeting with lobbyists to worry about such nonsense. Don't you know who I am?"

After the House Bank scandal, it seems, the public has come to understand that question—

and yes, they know who their congressmen are: arrogant, conceited, greedy, selfish and pompous politicians who are totally out of touch with the lives of the citizens they supposedly represent.

Now the nationwide term limits campaign gives ordinary citizens the chance to ask their congressmen the same question. And when Joe Average Voter asks his imperious Congressman, "Don't you know who I am," the sad fact is that the average incumbent hasn't a clue.

Congress today is lost in a perpetual re-election campaign that puts the typical incumbent in a cocoon of distorted reality and deception. All day members hear the demands of special interest groups. Campaign consultants design appeals to the political fringes and their schedulers send them over and over to the same corner of America—the corner with all the career politicians and lobbyists in it.

They Just Don't Get It

Usually, all they see is a reflection of themselves in the world of these professional flatterers and sycophants. It's no wonder that the most frequently expressed criticism of Congress is: "They just don't get it."

The continuing House Bank scandal proves that they still don't get it. As the scandal cripples a few and wounds many, the rest continue to play the game of politics as usual. Once again we hear campaign promises to rebuild the cities, balance the budget and punish the Japanese. They continue to blame the president, the courts and the public for every social and economic ill. Truly, they just don't get it.

The American public wants Congress to make difficult decisions. Decisions that might cause them to lose an election. Decisions that their consultants would counsel them against. Decisions that will help America.

But Congress, for too long, has had perpetual overdraft protection. This is the real scandal: Congress is a bank of bottomless promises. Promise the moon when there's nothing in your account. Promise reform when you know you're the one at fault. Promise the public anything, as long as you get re-elected.

Congress has been caught with a million bad checks—all those promises for all those years that they never meant to honor. The House Bank scandal has settled those old accounts. The House Bank with all the rubber checks has been closed.

Now it's time to close Congress with all those rubber promises.

Reprinted with permission of Gary Brookins.

Chapter Eight

Term Limits–

The Only Solution

The key to democracy is the importance of
"ruling and being ruled in turn."

—Aristotle.

Taking turns is a fundamental principle of any social or political structure. Without it, our lives would be chaos and civilization would collapse. We would be cannibals instead of citizens.

As young children, we are admonished by parents and teachers: "Let someone else have a turn on the swing." With the innocent selfishness of childhood we rebel, enjoying a moment of dominance and wanting more than all the others. But we are strictly instructed, "It isn't fair to be a hog."

In later life, we take turns at bat, at cleaning the dishes, at highway intersections and at the draft board. As adults, we alternate shifts at work, serve time on a jury or school committee, and take turns emptying the garbage. Andy Warhol even promises that we each get a turn at fame, but only 15 minutes' worth.

In nature, we see the same precept at work. Watch a flock of geese in flight. Each individual goose takes a turn leading the V-shaped skein, sharing the workload and collectively determining the course. Thus, leadership in nature has its own term limits. It's nature's way of maximizing the performance of a group and ensuring cooperation.

Human experience has taught us, however, that we cannot rely on Mother Nature to govern ourselves. Innocent childhood selfishness can quickly be transformed into tyranny, slavery and war. Thus we encode our most important social rules to protect us from our own worst instincts. We pass laws to preserve our rights, our freedoms and our control over government.

The question then becomes: "Should we have a law imposing term limits on our national legislators and, if so, what should it say and how should it be enacted?"

Americans, without doubt, understand the problem. In poll after poll, they say that Congress is out of control. Incumbents are exploiting their power to ensure their re-election: using the frank to brainwash the voters, funding wasteful pork barrel projects to bribe them, and jamming the airwaves with expensive commercials to deceive them.

The result: an unaccountable Congress that acts like a House of Lords. Out of touch and concerned only with re-election, its members ignore their responsibility to manage our government and plan for our nation's future. And yet our best citizens won't run for office because they know the system is rigged against them. Even as disgust with Congress rises to record levels, 98 percent of all incumbents get re-elected.

Limitations on congressional careers will lead to more competitive elections, more qualified candidates and more control over government. Successful citizens from all walks of life, not just lawyers, will be willing to run, because they'd have a chance, once again, to win—and winning would mean you could get something done, not that you'd have to wait 15 years to have enough seniority to have any real influence.

With more real citizens in our citizens legislature, we can expect and insist on a more efficient government, responsive programs and higher standards of public accountability.

Legislators won't be in office long enough to become corrupt and arrogant. In short, we can restore confidence in government again.

Imagine, for a moment, how different a citizens legislature would be in an era with term limits. Each new Congress would have over 200 new Members and, with half of all legislators unable or unwilling to seek re-election, the very nature of Congress would be changed.

Over the past 50 years, only those Congresses with large proportions of new Members, as in 1948, 1974 and 1980, brought forth meaningful changes, reforms and proposals to redirect and control the bureaucratic behemoth that government has become. Such dynamism and creativity would be the norm, not the exception, in a citizens legislature.

But even more dramatic would be the change in a Congress where half or more of the Members weren't running for re-election all the time.

Most current congressmen lament the present reality of the perpetual campaign—always looking for money, a quick press hit or a simplistic proposal that can be turned into a 20-second sound bite for television. They have to sell their souls to special interests to raise money for campaign ads and are afraid to do anything that might offend a lobbyist or powerful PAC. The result is a Congress in gridlock, trapped by the competing special interests who own the incumbents.

Suppose, instead, that half the members of Congress really have no future political ambitions. They are serving only for a few years, more conscious of their public duty than their political careers. And since they have no interest in fund-raising, public relations, propaganda and re-election strategy, they have the time to do their real job: Be a congressman.

They'll debate issues. They'll write their own speeches. They'll propose their own legislation and mark up their own bills. They'll take seriously the job of overseeing government, draft a responsible budget and, maybe, even visit the departments of the executive branch. (When's the last time a congressman or senator really went over to the Department of Agriculture to see what all those thousands of bureaucrats were doing?)

Term limitations will produce other reforms and benefits: The power of lobbyists and congressional staffs will be reduced, the seniority and retirement systems will be reformed, redundant committees will be consolidated, special interests will be curbed and the cozy old-boy network will be broken. Fairer elections will offer new opportunities for underrepresented political groups and local political party organizations will be fostered and revitalized.

Of course, no reform proposal is a panacea, and a congress with term limits will still reflect society's flaws. But term limitations will restore our power to correct a flawed institution, challenge the weak and remove the corrupt. It will make Congress better.

What Limits Should Be Enacted?

It is important, however, to consider what kind of term limits should be enacted. Some proposals currently under consideration contain loopholes that will almost certainly be exploited by careerist politicians.

There are three principal differences among the various bills that have been recommended or introduced in Congress to limit congressional terms: the number of terms to which members are limited; the question of consecutive vs. lifetime limits; and the inclusion of a grandfather clause.

Among proponents of term limits, there is general agreement that if the limits are to be effective, they must allow only short terms: two or three terms in the House and one or two terms in the Senate. A sizable proportion of those polled would prefer a one-term limit in each body, but many view the precedent of the 22nd Amendment (which limits the president to two terms) as an important consideration and feel, in any case, that a one-term limit would be too difficult to achieve politically, despite its merits.

There isn't much debate about the limit on tenure in the Senate. Almost everyone agrees that two terms are sufficient. When term limits were first proposed, there were many who assumed that twelve years would also be an appropriate limit in the House (*i.e.*, six terms). But in recent years, almost all principal public proponents have been advocating six- or eight-year limits in the House. Three terms is now the most widely supported recommendation. Americans, in general agree: Six years is enough!

As might be expected, members of Congress take a very different view. The overwhelming majority oppose any limit, despite clear evidence that their constituents disagree. Most of those who say they support term limits have co-sponsored watered-down bills that restrict tenure in each body to twelve or even 18 years in office.

Not only do these insipid proposals permit a dozen (or more) years in the House and then twelve (or more) years in the Senate, but they only count consecutive years against the limit.

Thus, a House member, under one proposal, could serve 18 years, take a two-year political appointment (as Ambassador to Bermuda, for example), and then start all over again. Most members wouldn't consider this too much of a hardship, as long as they can find a trustworthy seat warmer to hold their place while they're on sabbatical.

It is important, therefore, that a constitutional amendment limiting congressional terms stipulate a lifetime limit, as in the case of the presidential term limits. Six years in Congress, period. Otherwise, the limits would have almost no effect.

A Grandfather Clause?

The final question concerns whether current Members should be grand-fathered, that is, should their service prior to ratification of a term limits Amendment count against them. Some argue, as was the case in the referendum in Washington State in 1991, that a retroactive limit is necessary in order to move quickly to cure Congress of its careerism and incumbentitis.

But most proponents of limitations conclude that fighting against grandfather isn't very critical, since a term limits amendment, once enacted, would put such pressure on

Reprinted with permission of Tribune Media Services, Inc.

grandfathered members with long tenure that most would voluntarily retire. With thousands of new challengers each year and the dynamism of hundreds of freshmen in every Congress, the grandfathered bums who might want to hang around for a few more years would stick out like a sore thumb. The public would have no trouble kicking them out.

A retroactive proposal also seems unfair to many voters and to virtually all incumbents. The purpose of term limits, after all, is not to expel any individual congressman or senator, though many may deserve it. The goal is to reform the system so that, in the future, careerism is discouraged in the first place and legislators are discharged before they become corrupt and self-centered.

Given this analysis, it is clear that the struggle for meaningful term limits is headed for a confrontation. The public wants to limit legislators to six years or less in the House, and no more than two terms in the Senate. It also want lifetime limits or, at the very least, a provision that a politician who has reached his limit must take at least six years off before seeking office again. Members of Congress who support term limits, on the other hand, want longer limits with a two-year "out then back in" loophole. It should be an interesting fight.

The Amendment

On May 4, 1992, Americans to Limit Congressional Terms, on behalf of its 200,000 members, formally presented a proposed constitutional amendment to Congress. It is simple, succinct and unambiguous. It is of short duration and lifelong effect. It follows the precedent of the 22nd Amendment and has broad public support. Most importantly, it will produce a citizens legislature. It reads as follows:

RESOLVED, by the people of the United States of America . . . . .

No person who has been elected to the Senate two times shall be eligible for election or appointment to the Senate.

No person who has been elected to the House of Representatives three times shall be eligible for election to the House of Representatives.

Chapter Nine

Who Opposes Term Limits and What They're Up To

The American people want a constitution-al amendment limiting congressional terms. Every poll taken to date shows remarkably consistent and broad support for a return to a citizens legislature.

Gallup, ABC News, the *Wall St. Journal* and dozens of independent pollsters have found support for national term limits to range from 60 percent to more than 80 percent of those surveyed. Approval rates are essentially the same among Republicans and Democrats, blacks and whites, young and old, rich and poor. In short, it is not a partisan issue. Almost everyone agrees that we need to limit Congressional terms.

But some of the most powerful people and organizations in the country oppose term limits. The question is: Will they be able to thwart the will of the public? Do we have a government "of the people, by the people and for the people," or is it controlled by powerful incumbents, bureaucrats, lobbyists and special interests? The fight for term limits will ultimately provide the answer.

Opponents of term limits fall into five categories: incumbents, their staffs, lobbyists and special interests; government employees and their unions; and some sympathetic journalists in Washington. Each has placed self-interest ahead of national interest, and together they may prove to be a formidable and well-financed foe. To beat them, it's important to understand their motivation and the arguments they use.

It's no surprise that incumbent politicians oppose term limitation proposals. What is surprising is how deceptive and brazen their tactics have been.

Incumbents assert that only they have the wisdom and experience to be in Congress, but in truth they are terrified. The wife of one long-tenured House member admitted that there was "nothing else her husband could do," and without doubt no incumbent will be able to find work that provides the power, perks and royal lifestyle that so many of them have come to expect.

A survey of all 535 members of Congress in May 1992, found only 25 would sign a pledge supporting a constitutional amendment limiting congressional terms. Other members say they support term limits, but for many of them it's nothing more than strategic posturing in the face of an angry electorate.

The Republican Leadership in both the House and the Senate oppose limitations on terms. Of the 20 top congressional leaders, only one, Representative Newt Gingrich, has formally pledged to support term limits.

The story is largely the same in state capitals around the country. California Assembly Speaker Willie Brown, for example, raised $5 million from special interests to try to defeat the state term limits referendum in 1990. He failed.

Staffs are equally paranoid about term limits and lead the effort, behind the scenes, to derail the movement.

In Washington, staff members have assumed enormous power in Congress. Congressmen spend all their time courting the media and raising money, so the staff have become the real decisionmakers. Unelected and unbridled by the regulations that control other federal employees, they are modern-day Machiavellis, scheming to preserve their clout and control over the legislative agenda.

Term limits would destroy them. They thrive in the current system where they have two routes to power and prosperity: Either they can commit themselves to a member's career, gaining more and more influence over the years as he gains seniority and becomes too lazy or too worn out to worry about the details; or they can opt for the "in-and-out" approach, carefully winning some strategic position with a rising star member, and cashing in on their connections after a few years by becoming a lobbyist or joining a downtown law firm.

Term limits sabotages both options. The long careers will be gone and the power of their staffs, as well. And what law firm or client wants someone with yesterday's connections? These staffers know the big bucks come only if their connections stay in office.

A term-limited Congress wouldn't want so much staff anyway. Those 37,000 obsequious and devious gofers would just get in the way of a citizen legislator.

Freshmen members come to Congress like Jimmy Stewart arrived at the Senate in *Mr. Smith Goes to Washington*, expecting to give their own speeches, debate their own debates, decide their own positions, draft their own bills and cast their own votes. Time and again, freshmen congressmen have tried to reduce the power of staffs, and each time the powerful Committee chairmen stop them. With term limits, the staffs would be out.

Lobbyists and Special-Interest Groups

Lobbyists and other special interests are the ones financing the various campaigns against term limits. In Washington state, for example, a group called "No on 553" raised hundreds of thousands of dollars from such sources as the Philip Morris tobacco company, Kaiser Aluminum and the National Rifle Association. Hundreds of trial lawyers helped bankroll similar opposition efforts in California and Colorado.

Their motivation was candidly described by a veteran lobbyist in Washington: "We've spent millions buying the current power structure—we've got an investment we can't afford to give up."

Special interests are also worried that citizen legislators won't be bought so easily. They know that career politicians depend on lobbyists' money to pay for their re-election campaigns. Nothing would be worse, they know, than a Congress of citizens who weren't worried about getting re-elected.

Term limits would allow ordinary citizens to seriously consider running for Congress. Men and women with many different backgrounds, most of whom had already had a successful career in some other field, would run for office, hoping to serve a term or two in Congress. They wouldn't need to sell their souls to a lobbyist, nor would they want to. The golden age of the Washington lobbyist would be over.

Many government employees and especially the leaders of their unions also look at the term limitation movement with concern and anxiety. They know they have been living a charmed life. For decades, they have formed an incestuous relationship with congressional leaders, yielding to their wasteful gluttony and political whims in return for lifetime security and perpetual budgetary growth.

The bureaucrats, the lobbyists and the long-tenured congressional committee chairmen compose the elements of the infamous iron triangle of federal spending, waste and overregulation. Term limits threatens to destroy their whole carefully crafted empire.

The major government employee unions have been the principle sponsors of published attacks against term limits, such as those produced by long-time labor lobbyist, Vic Kamber. In many states, such as California, they are instructing their members to fight public referenda on term limits, at all costs. So far, their efforts have backfired, as most citizens see them as part of the problem, not part of the solution.

Inside-the-Beltway Journalists

Finally, there are the inside-the-Beltway journalists who wield their mighty pens in defense of career congressmen, claiming to know how Washington works, believe that term limits are an unrealistic dream of idealists who want to return to the primitive era of our Founding Fathers. The real motives are hidden behind the pompous platitudes of their prose.

First, many of them are political elitists afraid that the common folk will knock them off their own cozy pedestal. They are, after all, part of the political establishment and have developed over the years close ties to the politicians they cover. For decades, they have carefully cultivated their sources. Covering Congress (or should we say covering up for Congress?) has become simple: Contact a few sources, get a leak or two, and sell yourself as the ultimate insider.

Thus term limits will mean more work! They'll have hundreds of new outsiders to learn about, and no more easy access and simple scoops.

In addition, many of the Washington press corps are spouses, children or relatives of current or former members of Congress. Term limits undermines the legitimacy of their family business. How can ABC News congressional correspondent, Cokie Roberts, for example, be objective about congressional careerism when both her mother and father spent decades in Congress?

The Real Minority

There is one other group who are fighting against term limits: those who are happy with Congress. According to the most recent polls, 17 percent of the public thinks Congress is doing a good job. These people, presumably, believe that the nation is benefiting from the special-interest domination of Congress, the inability of Congress to control government waste and runaway spending, and the confusion, corruption and chaos that result from an unaccountable legislature whose laws promote endless litigation and social unrest. In other words, these people must be lawyers and consultants.

In summary, some of the country's most powerful—well-connected political operators, inside Washington and in positions of influence in our state capitals—are arguing against term limits. Their motivation, like that of our career congressmen, is their own self-interest. But many of them have come to realize that the idea of term limits is like a train that cannot be stopped. It will run them over and end their control of our government. In the meantime, there is only one thing they can do: Lie.

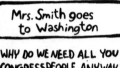

Chapter Ten

Lies, Lies, Lies
The Arguments Against Term Limits

Modern congressional politics is a monument to one thing: the Big Lie. And so it is from the opponents of term limits.

Any time you mention a congressman's name, you uncover the Big Lie. Everyone calls him "The Honorable." We all know it's not true. Other call him "Representative." Their noses grow even longer. And listen to them call *themselves* "public servants." Pinocchio would never be so bold!

The truth is that we're *their* servants. We do what they say and want—and they want to be in power forever.

The only real threat to their wonderful careers of political power and privilege is term limits. So naturally their defense is to lie about what term limits will do.

When a term limits referendum appeared on the ballot in Washington state last year, they said term limits would increase pollution, rob senior citizens and raise electric rates! The Exxon Valdez would drop anchor and spill oil in Puget Sound. And even worse, California would come up and steal all of Washington's water. Now, they've come up with even crazier arguments to confuse the public about the merits of a citizens legislature and the right of the public to change Congress.

Each argument is a lie, a big lie. But the bigger they are, the easier they fall when the public is given the facts.

★ *Big Lie Number 1: We need experienced Congressmen.*

Government is too complicated for amateurs who don't know their way around the Capitol. Only the seasoned veterans have the wisdom to guide our country.

Nonsense. If the government we've got is the result of all that experience, then let's have less!

Today's congressmen have the wrong kind of experience. Sure, they're experienced at holding fund-raisers and news conferences. They know how to avoid tough questions and speak in doubletalk. They're great at sending out franked propaganda and getting re-elected. But that's not the kind of experience we need.

Across this country there are hundreds of thousands of citizens who have real experience. They've raised families, paid taxes, run businesses and obeyed the law. They suffer with government regulations, inadequate schools, a crumbling infrastructure and declining community values.

They include engineers, teachers, scientists, doctors, builders, retailers, salesmen, programmers and people like you and me. Maybe Congress needs their experience to make government work better, instead of all the professional politicians and lawyers we've got there now.

★ *Big Lie Number 2: Term Limits aren't democratic.*

We should be free to choose whomever we want. Any congressman's term can be limited by the voters at the next election.

Democracy means that the people choose whom to vote for *and* how the elections are kept fair. Today, we have a system where the incumbents cheat and don't want anyone to stop them. The voters want to change the system, not just the incumbents.

The voters don't have a real choice in most elections anymore and feel helpless to defeat incumbents with all their special advantages. A Common Cause study shows that in the last election, 79 congressmen were unopposed, 158 were essentially unopposed (The challengers had less that $25,000.), and another 132 races were financially non-competitive (Incumbents spent more than twice as much as challengers.) Most voters just give up and don't even bother to vote.

In addition, the current system discourages ordinary people from running. Lawyers and career politicians are usually the only ones who become candidates now. Term limits will create five times as many open-seat elections, encouraging thousands of citizens to throw their hats into the ring. Then, elections will be real contests, attracting public interest and promoting voter participation. The voters will, at last, have some real choices.

★ *Big Lie Number 3: Term limits will make bureaucrats and lobbyists more powerful.*

Term limits will make the bureaucrats, the lobbyists and the congressional staff more powerful because all the rookies in Congress will need their help, fall for their tricks or succumb to their bribery.

First, how could it possibly get worse than it is now? We have ten times as many staff now as we did in the '50s and everyone agrees they have too much power; lobbyists like Charles Keating routinely win special favors from Congress that cost the taxpayers billions of dollars; and congressional oversight of the bureaucracy is a joke—it ought to be called overlooking, because so much is intentionally ignored.

In a Congress with term limits, excess staff would be the first thing to go. Freshmen Congressmen would want to write their own speeches, debate their own debates, and cast their own votes. It has always been the senior members, especially the committee chairmen, who expand staff and rely on their advice. Citizen legislators won't need them.

The bureaucrats and the lobbyists also depend on long-established relationships with the veteran politicians to look after their interests. New members in a Congress with term limits won't have any friends in the bureaucracy or play golf every weekend in a foursome of lobbyists. They'll be able to say **"no"** to the special interests and **"yes"** to real reforms in the way Congress works.

★ *Big Lie Number 4: We will lose great members of Congress.*

We'd lose a few great members of Congress if we had term limits. It's not fair to make these good guys leave.

We wouldn't lose them—they'd just get a chance to contribute in a different and maybe better way. Abraham Lincoln served only one term in Congress, for example. How many qualified presidential candidates stay in the House or Senate today, rather than move up, because they know they can stay in Congress forever? And besides, there are other ways to serve your country than as a politician. Who says a great Congressman can't become a great citizen. There is, after all, life after Congress.

Benjamin Franklin said it best:

> In free governments the rulers are the servants, and their people their superiors. . . . For the former to return among the latter [does] not degrade, but promote them.

And let's not forget how the current incumbency protection systems deprives our Congress of thousands of citizens who may possess even greater talents. We can point to only a very few legislative giants in our current Congress. With term limits, surely there would be many more.

★ *Big Lie Number 5: We Already Have Turnover.*

We don't need term limits because we already have lots of turnover. Look at all the resignations this year and the prospect of 100 or more new faces next year. Elections already give us all the term limits we need.

Almost all the turnover in Congress occurs because of five factors: Death, illness, redistricting, running for higher office and resignation because of scandal, indictment or arrest. In 1992, there is one additional factor: Congress passed a special loophole allowing members who retire this year to transfer the money in their campaign accounts into personal bank accounts!

In short, the turnover we now have is turnover at the pleasure of the incumbents. They leave when they want to! Our Founding Fathers expected that the voters would decide when incumbents left office—and for more than a century that was the way it worked. Now, the voters are almost powerless unless there's a huge scandal like the House Bank affair.

Certainly Americans are pleased that many career politicians are leaving Congress this year, because of the combined effects of redistricting (which happens only once a decade), the various congressional scandals and the aforementioned take-the-money-and-run retirement incentive. Many are hopeful that these scandals will help defeat as many as 30 or 40 more. But still, they want term limits.

The voters are angry and want to do two things. First, kick the bums out of Congress (or let them kick themselves out). Second, limit the terms of the new batch of politicians so they don't turn into bums, too.

★ *Big Lie Number 6: It's all a Republican plot.*

It's just a Republican plot. The Democrats have controlled Congress for nearly 40 years and the Republicans see this as the only way to gain control.

Among the public, more term limits supporters are Democrats than Republicans. Hundreds of leading Democrats, including Harry Truman, John Kennedy, John Lindsay and Jerry Brown have advocated term limits.

There is, of course, no reason why the seat of a departing congressman, forced to retire because of term limits, would be won by a Republican instead of a Democrat, unless he and his ideas were more attractive to the voters. In addition, many Democratic supporters of term limits feel that their party has become rigid and uncompetitive. Term limits, they say, would reinvigorate a brain-dead party.

The real opponents of term limits are not Republicans or Democrats, but incumbents of both parties. If the Republicans had controlled Congress for the past 38 years instead of the Democrats, the situation would be no different. They would have become corrupted by power as absolutely as the Democrats have been.

Oddly enough, in states with Republican-controlled legislatures, it's called a Democratic plot. Of course it isn't a plot at all. It's simply the people, pleading for control of their Congress—trying to take it back from career politicians of both parties.

★ *Big Lie Number 7: Nothing will change.*

It won't make any difference. Term limits will only bring in new politicians with new faces but all the same problems. Term limits is treating a symptom, not the disease.

Careerism in politics is the disease. Incumbentitis is its name. Term limits are the only cure.

Everything else that corrupts our political system and our Congress is a result of this sickness. It is what corrupts the minds of our legislators. It causes them to change the way they think, act and vote.

Instead of asking, "What should I do to help my country?" the professional incumbent asks, "What do I do to get re-elected?" From that, flows every missed budget, wasteful program and campaign trick. Incumbentitis distorts elections, extorts special interests and deceives the voter.

Any effort to cure this disease with so-called campaign reforms, spending limits, new rules for using the frank, staffs or other perquisites or even public financing are doomed to failure. The professional politicians in Congress never have and never will vote for rules that help challengers more than incumbents. Any new reform will have loopholes that only they can exploit and lead, in the end, only to more of the same: a Capitol filled with congressmen-for-life.

The goal of term limits is to cure this disease, not to just change a few faces. True relief comes by bringing to Washington people with new faces and new minds. Their goal won't be to build a career, but to save a country.

The biggest lie of all is that the incumbents know what the voters want. They don't.

They've lost all touch with the real America.
The sad truth is: They just don't get it.

Chapter Eleven

Conclusion:

Ten Things You Can Do to Help Enact Term Limits

Placing term limits on Congress isn't going to be easy. The incumbent politicians, as we have seen, will lie, cheat and even steal to preserve their privileges, perquisites and power.

But maybe Congress will decide, for once, to do the right thing. In a matter of only a few weeks, it could hold hearings on term limits and vote for a resolution to amend the Constitution. Within a few months, 38 states would ratify the Amendment and it would become the 28th Amendment to our Constitution.

Sadly, Congress refuses to do the right thing. Therefore we have only the much more difficult path of state-by-state referenda and gradual pressure on Congress. But before long, we will succeed.

Organizations have been established in every major referendum state to push for term limits (see Appendix One) and other groups are being formed in non-referendum states to build support for local legislative efforts. Nearly a quarter of a million Americans have joined Americans to Limit Congressional Terms. This revolution has begun and will not be stopped. And here are ten important things you can do to help!

1. Join ALCT today. Call 1-800-6IS-ENUF for information and a membership application.

2. Organize a meeting of ALCT members in your community or congressional district. ALCT headquarters will be happy to help with mailing labels, speakers, etc.

3. Support a local "Take-the-Pledge" program. Have your friends and neighbors contact all candidates for Congress in your area to see if they support term limits—and, if so, what kind and for how long. Forward copies of signed pledges and other written responses to ALCT headquarters.

PLEDGE TO LIMIT
CONGRESSIONAL TERMS

I, _____, a member of Congress for the state of _____, pledge to my constituents and to the American people, an overwhelming majority of whom support limiting the length of time a citizen may serve in Congress, that I will:

ONE, To the best of my ability, reflect the will of the people and support efforts in the United States Congress to limit by constitutional amendment, the length of time any citizen may serve in the United States House of Representatives and the United States Senate; and

TWO, Support every effort, whether by resolution in the state legislature, by citizen initiative or by referendum, to call upon my colleagues in Congress to limit in a constitutional manner the length of time a citizen may serve in the United States House of Representatives and United States Senate.

_____
Signature

Date: _____

4. Persuade undecided candidates to support term limits. ALCT's Political Activity Division will help you convince hesitant candidates that support for a citizen legislature is a critical political credential.

5. Circulate a petition among your neighbors. It should urge Congress to debate and vote on a term limits amendment. ALCT will provide pre-printed petition forms and personally deliver your petition to the Congressman and Senators from your area.

An organization in your area (see Appendix One) is probably circulating a petition in your area to persuade Congress that the people want term limitations. If you can't hook up with on ongoing petition campaign, start your own! On the next two pages is a petition form that you can use at shopping centers, door-to-door or at citizens' group meetings.

Petition
from the Citizens of

We the People, all voters in the _____ district of the State of _____, petition our Representative and Senators in Congress to enact an Amendment to the Constitution of the United States, as follows:

No person who has been elected to the Senate two times shall be eligible for election or appointment to the Senate.

No person who has been elected to the House of Representatives three times shall be eligible for election to the House of Representatives.

Signature of Registered Voter   Address   Telephone

_____

_____

_____

_____

Signature of Registered Voter   Address   Telephone

_____

_____

_____

_____

_____

_____

_____

_____

_____

_____

_____

**Send to Americans to Limit Congressional Terms
1050 Langley Hill Drive, Langley, Virginia 22101**

6. Work for passage of your state's referendum. If your state has a referendum on term limits on the ballot, ask for a Referendum Support Package from ALCT. It'll provide materials you can distribute to explain the referendum to friends and neighbors. Join a referendum get-out-the-vote campaign. Phone banks will be set up a few weeks before each state referendum and people are needed to hand out information and voter guides on Election Day.

7. Contribute to ALCT's Term Limits Education Campaign. Money will be used to educate millions of voters about term limits, pending referenda and the proposed constitutional amendment limiting congressional terms.

8. Help form a local Term Limits Advocacy Group. ALCT's National Advocacy Group will help you contact radio talk shows, public debate forums and newspaper editors as a grass-roots spokesperson for the term limits movement.

9. If you live in a non-referendum state, meet with your state legislators to help identify term limits supporters. ALCT will coordinate meetings with legislative leaders in your state Capitol.

10. Show off your support for term limits with ALCT bumper stickers, decals

and T-shirts. Your parked car can become an ally in the term limits fight.

The one thing that all of us must continue to do is talk and write about term limits. Term limits opponents want this issue to go away. They want us to forget about our anger and tire of the struggle. Many of them will promise to reform and pledge to start listening to the average citizen.

This year's House Bank scandal has forced an unusually large number of members to retire and some have even been defeated. The survivors in Congress will now say that the bums have already been kicked out. Don't believe them!

Without term limits, every new member of Congress will soon want to become a congressman-for-life. The temptations of power, privilege and perquisites will always be there and, before long, new bums will be back.

That's why we all have to keeping talking about term limits. It's our only real weapon— straight talk about Congress and what it should be.

Wherever you are—you can talk about term limits: in church, at the dinner table, with co-workers or at the local community center. Whenever you hear anyone discussing politics, elections, the presidential campaign or just their frustration with Washington—offer the only real solution: a citizens legislature.

We've all been fooled for too long. Politicians have been promising and promising and promising. Their credo is: Say whatever has to be said to get re-elected. This year many of them are even saying that they aren't really politicians.

Politician Detection Kit

In self-defense, maybe we can persuade the pharmaceutical companies to provide, as a public service, some sort of politician detection kit—like the pregnancy detection kits that were recently developed. It might be a small bottle with a rubber tube into which a suspected politician blows a mouthful of his own hot air. Inside the jar would be a clear plastic capsule that turns brown if it detects the scent of nascent careerism in the suspect's exhalation. True citizen legislators would get a clear sign of approval.

Unfortunately, such a simple diagnostic device is unlikely. Instead we offer our own test for unbridled ambition, the disease of modern politics. Next time you're confronted with a candidate for Congress, give him or her this simple examination:

KICK THE BUMS OUT!

A TEST FOR CITIZEN LEGISLATORS

Question and point calculation:

1. How many years served in Congress? _____ Points = (number of years)^2

2. How many years on Congressional staff? _____ Points = 3 x (number of years)

3. How many years as state legislator? _____ Points = 2 x (number of years)

4. How many years in other elected office? _____ Points = 1 x (number of years)

5. Attend Law School? _____ Points=10 if Yes

6. How long practicing law? _____ 10 points if 2 yrs.; 5 points if more than 2 years.

7. How many years with full-time job with no political connection? _____ Points = -(number of years)/2

8. How many years as business owner? _____ Points = -(number of years)

9. How many years married? _____ Points = -(number of years)/3

10. How many years with children in house? _____ Points = -(number of years)

11. How many years dreaming of politics? _____ Points = 2 x (number of years)

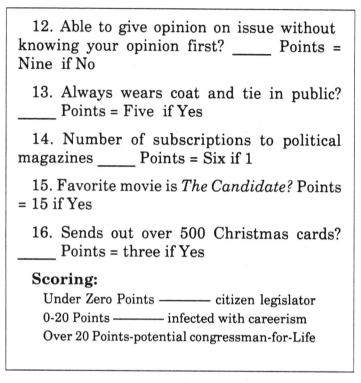

12. Able to give opinion on issue without knowing your opinion first? _____ Points = Nine if No

13. Always wears coat and tie in public? _____ Points = Five if Yes

14. Number of subscriptions to political magazines _____ Points = Six if 1

15. Favorite movie is *The Candidate?* Points = 15 if Yes

16. Sends out over 500 Christmas cards? _____ Points = three if Yes

Scoring:
Under Zero Points ———— citizen legislator
0-20 Points ———— infected with careerism
Over 20 Points-potential congressman-for-Life

This test may help us spot good new candidates for Congress, but it won't really give them much help this year in getting elected. The cards are all stacked against them, and only when they're running against an incumbent who's been crippled by scandal are they likely to achieve victory.

Fortunately, Americans aren't quitters. Many of us have tried for years to change Congress. For most, it's been a frustrating struggle, but now we understand the real problem—the career politician who doesn't want to leave, doesn't want to act and doesn't want to change.

At last we've rediscovered the means to reform Congress and restore our democracy. We have again declared our independence and launched an historic battle for self-government. The Second American Revolution has begun.

Before long term limits will win and we'll kick the bums out—for good.

Appendix One

Term Limitation Organizations

National

Americans to Limit Congressional
Terms
1050 Langley Hill Dr.
Langley, Virginia 22101
(703) 821-5455

Alabama

David Donaldson
P.O. Box 530390
Birmingham, AL 35253
(205)877-3021

Alaska

Fritz Pettyjohn
P.O. Box 110912
Anchorage, AK 99511
(907) 345-5174

Limit '92 (State limitations)
P.O. Box 242592
Anchorage, AK 99524
(907) 561-1265

Arizona

Citizens for Limited Terms
4700 Central Avenue
Suite 121
Phoenix, AZ 85014
(602) 265-0544

Arizona Citizens for Congressional Reform
Al Walther
P.O. Box 11707
Prescott, AZ 86304
(602) 445-0874

Arkansas

Arkansans for Governmental Reform
Steve Munn
P.O. Box 1447
Little Rock, AR 72203
(501) 661-8699

California

California Committee to Limit Terms
Ted Costa
3385 Arden Way
Sacramento, CA 95825
(916) 482-6175

Foundation for Citizen Representation
Pete Schabarum
880 West 1st St. Unit 612
Los Angeles, CA 90012
(213) 617-3874

Connecticut

Tom Durso
P.O. Box 571
Watertown, CT 06795
(203) 274-4650

Florida

Eight is Enough
Phil Handy/John Sowinski
P.O. Box 4888
Orlando, FL 32802
(407) 839-5888

Georgia

Glen Hicks
3352 Lower Doug Gap Road
Dalton, GA 30720
(404) 278-6514

Idaho

Citizens for Political Reform
P.O. Box 836
Boise, ID 83701
(208) 336-4449

Maine

Mainers Back in Charge
27 Danford St.
Norway, ME 04268
(207) 743-9129

Massachusetts

LIMITS
Dorothea Thomas-Vitrac
P.O. Box 2432
Worcester, MA 01613
508/752-0720

Michigan

Campaign to Limit Politicians' Terms

Tim Purdy/Tish Berkey
4616 44th Street, S.E.
Grand Rapids, MI 49512
(616) 957-2177

Minnesota

Minnesotans for Term Limits

Ben Whitney
1900 Foshay Tower, 821 Marquette
Minneapolis, MN 55402
(612) 337-5536

Missouri

Missourians for Limited Terms

John Thompson
P.O. Box 317
Marshfield, MO 65706
(800) 473-TERM

Montana

Montanans for Term Limitation

Ron Oberlander
P.O. Box 164
Calispell, MT 59903
(406) 257-2400

Nebraska

Nebraskans for Term Limits
Ed Jaksha
P.O. Box 57193
Lincoln, NE 68505

New Hampshire

Senator Gordon Humphrey
State House
Concord, NH 03301
(603) 271-1110

New Jersey

REVOLT
Tom Blomquist
P.O. Box 989
Brick, NJ 08723
(908) 892-1518

New Mexico

State Representative
Mark Caruso
4302 Carlisle NE
Albuquerque, NM 87107
(505) 883-5000

North Carolina

Jay Kriss
P.O. Box 975
Smithfield, NC 27577
(919) 989-7676

Louis March
Dean Witter Building
4700 Six Forks Road
Raleigh, NC 27609 (919) 781-1100

North Dakota

**North Dakotans for Better
Government**
Kent French
P.O. Box 2074
Bismark, ND 58502
(701) 255-1705

Ohio

**Coalition of Ohioans to Limit
Terms**
Cliff Arnebeck
65 E. State Street
Columbus, OH 43215
(614) 481-0669

Ohioans for Term Limits
John Jazwa
12500 Elmwood Avenue
Cleveland, OH 44111
(216) 671-0210

Oregon

LIMITS
Frank Eisenzimmer
19021 SE Division, Suite C
Gresham, OR 97030
(503) 667-8315 (503) 665-4142

Pennsylvania

Pennsylvanians for Term Limits
RD 5, Box 156
Blairsville, PA 15715
(412) 244-4081
(412) 459-8247

South Carolina

Carter Hardwick
616 Harbor City Place
Charleston, SC 24912
(803) 795-3118

South Dakota

South Dakotans for Limited Terms
Jeff Hayzlett
P.O. Box 1684
Sioux Falls, SD 57101
(605) 338-6621

Texas

Texans for Term Limitation
Rob Mosbacher
P.O. Box 1906
Houston, TX 77251
(713) 546-2545

Virginia

Virginians for Term Limits
Kristine Kirby
8123 Heatherton Lane, Suite 201
Vienna, VA 22180
(804) 353-4554

Washington

LIMIT
Sherry Bockwinkel
P.O. Box 98003
Tacoma, WA 98498
(206) 759-7320

Wisconsin

Badgers Back in Charge
Kevin Hermening
P.O. Box 1992
Freedom, WI 54131
(715) 693-3018

Wyoming

Wyomingites for Citizen Government
Dave Dawson
P.O. Box 4322
Casper, WY 82604
(307) 237-1431

Appendix Two

===

Congressional Overdrafts

ALABAMA

Bevill, Tom (D)	4
Brower, Glen (D)	0
Callahan, Sonny (R)	9
Cramer, Robert E. Jr. (D)	11
Dickinson, William (R)	0
Erdreich, Ben (D)	0
Harris, Claude (D)	0

ALASKA

Young, Don (R)	57

ARIZONA

Kolbe, Jim (D)	0
Kyl, Jon (R)	0
Pastor, Ed (D)	0
Rhodes, John J. III	32
Stump, Bob (R)	0

ARKANSAS

Alexander, Bill (D)	487

Anthony, Beryl Jr., (D)	409
Hammerschmidt, John P. (R)	224
Thornton, Ray (D)	1

CALIFORNIA

Anderson, Glenn M. (D)	3
Beilenson, Anthony C. (D)	5
Berman, Howard L. (D)	67
Boxer, Barbara (D)	143
Brown, George (D)	26
Campbell, Tom (R)	4
Condit, Gary (D)	4
Cox, C. Christopher (R)	0
Cunningham, Randy (R)	1
Dannemayer, William (R)	26
Dellums, Ron (D)	851
Dixon, Julian (D)	0
Dooley, Calvin (D)	0
Doolittle, John T. (R)	0
Dornan, Robert (R)	0
Dreier, David (R)	0
Dymally, Mervyn (D)	1
Edwards, Don (D)	13
Fazio, Vic (D)	0
Gallegly, Elton (R)	5
Herger, Wally (R)	0
Hunter, Duncan (R)	399
Lagomarsin, Robert (R)	3
Lantos, Tom (D)	0
Lehman, Richard (D)	10
Levine, Mel (D)	0
Lewis, Jerry (R)	0

Lowery, Bill (R)	300
Martinez, Matthew (D)	19
Matsui, Robert (D)	25
McCandless, Alfred (R)	0
Miller, George (D)	99
Mineta, Norman (D)	3
Moorhead, Carlos (R)	0
Packard, Ronald (R)	4
Panetta, Leon (D)	12
Pelosi, Nancy (D)	28
Riggs, Frank (R)	3
Rohrabacher, Dana (R)	8
Roybal, Edward (D)	11
Stark, Fortney (D)	64
Thomas, William (R)	119
Torres, Esteban (D)	0
Waters, Maxine (D)	5
Waxman, Henry (D)	434

COLORADO

Allard, Wayne (R)	0
Campbell, Ben Nighthorse (D)	0
Hefley, Joel (R)	3
Schaefer, Daniel (R)	6
Schroeder, Patricia (D)	5
Skags, David (D)	57

CONNECTICUT

DeLauro, Rosa (D)	0
Franks, Gary (R)	7
Gejdenson, Sam (D)	51
Johnson, Nancy (R)	2
Kennelly, Barbara (D)	60

Shays, Christopher (R)	18

DELAWARE

Carper, Thomas (D)	3

FLORIDA

Bacchus, Jim (D)	3
Bennett, Charles (D)	4
Bilirakis, Michael (R)	0
Fascell, Dante (D)	1
Gibbons, Sam (D)	0
Goss, Porter (R)	0
Hutto, Earl (D)	1
Ireland, Andy (R)	38
James, Craig (R)	0
Johnston, Harry (D)	1
Lehman, William (D)	0
Lewis, Tom (R)	8
McCollum, Bill (R)	0
Peterson, Douglas (D)	0
Ros-Lehtinen, Ileana (R)	0
Shaw, E. Clay (R)	0
Smith, Larence (D)	161
Stearns, Clifford (R)	9
Young, C.W. Bill (R)	0

GEORGIA

Barnard, Doug (D)	30
Darden, George (D)	35
Gingrich, Newt (R)	22
Hatcher, Charles (D)	819
Jenkins, Ed (D)	0
Jones, Ben (D)	7

Lewis, John (D)   125

Ray, Richard (D)   1

Rowland, J. Roy (D)   0

Thomas, Lindsay (D)   6

HAWAII

Abercrombie, Neil (D)   0

Mink, Patsy (D)   0

IDAHO

LaRocco, Larry (D)   0

Stallings, Richard (D)   8

ILLINOIS

Annunzio, Frank (D)   0

Bruce, Terry (D)   2

Collins, Cardiss (D)   18

Costello, Jerry (D)   1

Cox, John (D)   0

Crane, Philip (R)   0

Durbin, Richard (D)   12

Evans, Lane (D)   9

Ewing, Thomas (R)   0

Fawell, Harris (R)   0

Hastert, J. Dennis (R)   44

Hayes, Charles (D)   716

Hyde, Henry (R)   2

Lipinski, William (D)   2

Michel, Robert (R)   0

Porter, John Edward (R)   1

Poshard, Glenn (D)   0

Rostenkowski, Dan (D)   0

Russo, Marty (D)   4

Sangmeister, George (R)	0
Savage, Gus (D)	4
Yates, Sidney (D)	4

INDIANA

Burton, Dan (R)	0
Hamilton, Lee (D)	0
Jacobs, Andy (D)	1
Jontz, Jim (D)	4
Long, Jill (D)	21
McCloskey, Frank (D)	65
Myers, John (R)	61
Roemer, Tim (D)	0
Sharp, Philip (D)	120
Viclosky, Peter (D)	0

IOWA

Grandy, Fred (R)	0
Leach, Jim (R)	0
Lightfoot, Jim (R)	105
Nagle, David (D)	4
Nussle, Jim (R)	0
Smith, Neal (D)	2

KANSAS

Glickman, Dan (D)	105
Meyers, Jan (R)	0
Nichols, Dick (R)	0
Roberts, Pat (R)	4
Slattery, Jim (D)	50

KENTUCKY

Bunning, Jim (R)	0
Hopkins, Larry (R)	83

Hubbard, Carroll (D)	152
Mazzoli, Romano (D)	0
Natcher, William (D)	0
Perkins, Carl C. (D)	514
Rogers, Harold (R)	0

LOUISIANA

Baker, Richard (R)	6
Hayes, James (D)	0
Holloway, Clyde (R)	10
Huckaby, Jerry (D)	88
Jefferson, William (D)	8
Livingston, Bob (R)	0
McCrery, Jim (R)	0
Tauzin, W.J. (D)	5

MAINE

Andrews, Thomas (D)	0
Snowe, Olympia (R)	1

MARYLAND

Bentley, Helen (R)	0
Byron, Beverly (D)	6
Cardin, Benjamin (D)	0
Gilchrest, Wayne (R)	0
Hoyer, Steny (D)	3
McMillen, C. Thomas (D)	0
Mfume, Kweisi (D)	12
Morella, Constance (R)	0

MASSACHUSETTS

Atkins, Chester (D)	127
Donnelly, Brian (D)	70
Early, Joseph D. (D)	140

Frank, Barney (D)	0
Kennedy, Joseph (D)	0
Markey, Edward (D)	92
Mavroules, Nicholas (D)	1
Moakley, John Joseph (D)	90
Neal, Richard (D)	87
Olver, John (D)	0
Studds, Gerry (D)	10

MICHIGAN

Bonior, David (D)	76
Broomfield, William S. (R)	0
Camp, David (R)	6
Carr, Bob (D)	1
Collins, Barbara-Rose (D)	0
Conyers, John Jr. (D)	273
Davis, Robert W. (R)	878
Dingell, John (D)	48
Ford, William (D)	6
Henry, Paul (R)	20
Hertel, Dennis (D)	547
Kildee, Dale (D)	100
Levin, Sander (D)	0
Pursell, Carl (R)	17
Traxler, Bob (D)	201
Upton, Fred (R)	1
Vander Jagt, Guy (R)	0
Wolpe, Howard (D)	8

MINNESOTA

Oberstar, James (D)	2
Penny, Timothy (D)	7
Peterson, Collin (D)	0

Ramstad, Jim (R)   5
Sabo, Martin (D)   0
Sikorski, Gerry (D)   697
Vento, Bruce (D)   3
Weber, Vin (R)   125

MISSISSIPPI

Espy, Mike (D)   191
Montgomery, G.V. (D)   0
Parker, Mike (D)   13
Taylor, Gene (D)   14
Whitten, Jamie (D)   0

MISSOURI

Clay, William L. (D)   328
Coleman, E. Thomas (R)   0
Emerson, Bill (R)   6
Gephardt, Richard (D)   28
Hancock, Mel (R)   0
Horn, Joan Kelly (D)   1
Skelton, Ike (D)   9
Volkmer, Harold (D)   1
Wheat, Alan (D)   86

MONTANA

Marlenee, Ron (R)   20
William, Pat (D)   66

NEBRASKA

Barrett, Bill (R)   0
Bereuter, Douglas (R)   39
Hoagland, Peter (D)   0

NEVADA

Bilbray, James (D)   0

Vucanovich, Barbara (R)   2

NEW HAMPSHIRE

Swett, Dick (D)   1

Zeliff, William (R)   0

NEW JERSEY

Andrews, Robert (D)   0

Dwyer, Bernard (D)   10

Gallo, Dean (R)   2

Guarini, Frank (D)   0

Hughes, William (D)   0

Pallone, Frank (D)   0

Payne, Donald (D)   6

Rinaldo, Matthew (R)   8

Roe, Robert (D)   6

Roukema, Marge (R)   5

Saxton, Jim (R)   2

Smith, Christopher (R)   0

Torricelli, Robert (D)   27

Zimmer, Dick (R)   0

NEW MEXICO

Richardson, Bill (D)   6

Schiff, Steven (R)   1

Skeen, Joe (R)   0

NEW YORK

Ackerman, Gary (D)   111

Boehlert, Sherwood (R)   1

Downey, Thomas (D)   151

Engel, Eliot (D)	21
Fish, Hamilton (R)	0
Flake, Floyd (D)	3
Gilman, Benjamin (R)	0
Green, Bill (R)	10
Hochbrueckner, George (D)	49
Horton, Frank (R)	3
Houghton, Amo (R)	0
LaFalce, John (D)	0
Lent, Norman (R)	0
Lowey, Nita (D)	1
Manton, Thomas (D)	17
Martin, David (R)	8
McGrath, Raymond (R)	4
McHugh, Matthew (D)	1
McNulty, Michael (D)	15
Molinari, Susan (R)	5
Mrazek, Robert (D)	920
Nowak, Henry (D)	0
Owens, Major (D)	48
Paxon, L. William (R)	96
Rangel, Charles (D)	64
Scheuer, James (D)	133
Schumer, Charles (D)	0
Serrano, Jose (D)	7
Slaughter, Louise McIntosh (D)	0
Solarz, Stephen (D)	743
Solomon, Gerald (R)	20
Towns, Edophus (D)	408
Walsh, James (R)	34
Weiss, Ted (D)	3

NORTH CAROLINA

Ballenger, Cass (R)	0
Coble, Howard (R)	0
Hefner, W.G. Bill (D)	0
Jones, Walter (D)	63
Lancaster, H. Martin (D)	5
Mcmillan, J. Alex (R)	4
Neal, Stephen (D)	7
Price, David (D)	8
Rose, Charlie (D)	0
Taylor, Charles (R)	0
Valentine, Tim (D)	5

NORTH DAKOTA

Dorgan, Byron (D)	98

OHIO

Applegate, Douglas (D)	0
Boehner, John (R)	0
Eckart, Dennis (D)	0
Feighan, Edward (D)	397
Gillmor, Paul (R)	0
Gradison, Willis (R)	1
Hall, Tony (D)	0
Hobson, David (R)	0
Kaptur, Marcy (D)	0
Kasich, John (R)	0
Luken, Charles (D)	0
McEwen, Bob (R)	166
Miller, Clarence (R)	0
Oakar, Mary Rose (D)	213
Oxley, Michael (R)	6
Pease, Donald (D)	0

Regula, Ralph (R)	14
Sawyer, Thomas (D)	0
Stokes, Louis (D)	551
Traficant, James (D)	0
Wylie, Chalmers (R)	515

OKLAHOMA

Brewster, William (D)	2
Edwards, Mickey (R)	386
English, Glenn (D)	1
Inhofe, James (R)	0
McCurdy, Dave (D)	8
Synar, Mike (D)	11

OREGON

AuCoin, Les (D)	83
DeFazio, Peter (D)	0
Kopetski, Michael (D)	0
Smith, Robert (R)	0
Wyden, Ron (D)	0

PENNSYLVANIA

Blackwell, Lucien (D)	0
Borski, Robert (D)	33
Clinger, William (R)	0
Coughlin, Lawrence (R)	1
Coyne, William (D)	0
Foglietta, Thomas (D)	0
Gaydos, Joseph (D)	3
Gekas, George (R)	0
Goodling, William (R)	430
Kanjorski, Paul (D)	7
Kolter, Joe (D)	0

Kostmayer, Peter (D)	50
McDade, Joseph (R)	0
Murphy, Austin (D)	6
Murtha, John (D)	10
Ridge, Thomas (R)	2
Ritter, Don (R)	0
Santorum, Rick (R)	0
Schulze, Richard (R)	4
Shuster, Bud (R)	32
Walker, Robert (R)	0
Weldon, Curtis (R)	9
Yatron, Gus (D)	0

RHODE ISLAND

Machtley, Ronald (R)	21
Reed, Jack (D)	0

SOUTH CAROLINA

Derrick, Butler (D)	0
Patterson, Elizabeth (D)	2
Ravenel, Arthur (R)	0
Spence, Floyd (R)	12
Spratt, John (D)	46
Tallon, Robin (D)	2

SOUTH DAKOTA

Johnson, Tim (D)	0

TENNESSEE

Clement, Bob (D)	1
Cooper, Jim (D)	7
Duncan, John (R)	0
Ford, Harold (D)	388
Gordon, Bart (D)	6

Lloyd, Marilyn (D)	8
Quillen, James (R)	0
Sundquist, Don (R)	2
Tanner, John (D)	3

TEXAS

Andrews, Michael (D)	121
Archer, Bill (R)	1
Armey, Dick (R)	19
Barton, Joe (R)	0
Brooks, Jack (D)	0
Bryant, John (D)	55
Bustamante, Albert (D)	30
Chapman, Jim (D)	0
Coleman, Ronald (D)	673
Combest, Larry (R)	0
de la Garza, Kika (D)	284
DeLay, Tom (R)	11
Edwards, Chet (D)	0
Fields, Jack (R)	22
Frost, Martin (D)	0
Geren, Pete (D)	3
Gonzalez, Henry (D)	0
Hall, Ralph (D)	18
Johnson, Sam (R)	0
Laughlin, Greg (D)	9
Ortiz, Solomon (D)	18
Pickle, J.J. (D)	0
Sarpalius, Bill (D)	6
Smith, Lamar (R)	1
Stenholm, Charles (D)	86
Washington, Craig (D)	3

Wilson, Charles (D)	81

UTAH

Hansen, James (R)	0
Orton, Bill (D)	0
Owens, Wayne (D)	87

VERMONT

Sanders, Bernard (I)	5

VIRGINIA

Allen, Geroge (R)	0
Bateman, Herbert (R)	0
Bliley, Thomas (R)	0
Boucher, Rick (D)	1
Moran, James (D)	3
Olin, Jim (D)	1
Payne, L. F. (D)	0
Pickett, Owen (D)	1
Sisisky, Norman (D)	0
Wolf, Frank (R)	0

WASHINGTON

Chandler, Rod (R)	1
Dicks, Norman (D)	3
Foley, Thomas (D)	2
McDermott, Jim (D)	0
Miller, John (R)	58
Morrison, Sid (R)	0
Swift, Al (D)	0
Unsoeld, Jolene (D)	1

WEST VIRGINIA

Mollohan, Alan (D)	12

Rahall, Mick Joe II (D)	0
Staggers, Harley (D)	0
Wise, Robert (D)	0

WISCONSIN

Aspin, Les (D)	6
Gunderson, Steve (R)	22
Kleczka, Gerald (D)	1
Klug, Scott (R)	3
Moody, Jim (D)	0
Obey, David (D)	64
Petri, Thomas (R)	77
Roth, Toby (R)	0
Sensenbrenner, James (R)	14

WYOMING

Thomas, Craig (R)	0

AMERICAN SAMOA

Faleomavaega, Eni (D)	63

DISTRICT OF COLUMBIA

Norton, Eleanor Holmes (D)	0

GUAM

Blaz, Ben (R)	36

PUERTO RICO

Colorado, Antonio (D)	0

VIRGIN ISLANDS

de Lugo, Ron (D)	106

FORMER MEMBERS

Baddam, Robert (R)	45
Bates, Jim (D)	89
Bosco, Douglas (D)	124
Brown, Senator Hank (R)	18
Cheney, Dick (R) [Sec. of Defense]	25
Coats, Senator Dan (R)	3
Coelho, Tony (D)	316
Craig, Senator Larry (R)	9
DeWine, Michael (R) [Ohio Lt. Gov.]	9
Fauntroy, Walter (D)	145
Flippo, Ronnie (D)	17
Grant, Bill (R)	106
Gray, Kenneth (R)	19
Gray, William (D)	60
Kemp, Jack (R) [Sec. of HUD]	1
Lukens, Donald (R)	142
Madigan, Edward (R) [Sec. of Agriculture]	49
Martin, Lynn (R) [Sec. of Labor]	16
Robinson, Tommy (R)	996
Rowland, John (R)	108
Udall, Morris (D)	128
Walgren, Doug (D)	858
Wright, James (D) [former Speaker]	138